Experiencing God

Contents

Introduction

The writings of the eighteenth-century American theologian and philosopher Jonathan Edwards (1703–1758) are being studied with increasing urgency by Christians throughout the world in the 1990s.

Edwards studied at Yale and then became a minister of the Congregational Church, Northampton, Massachusetts. Between 1734 and 1747 he became a leading figure in the American religious revival which became known as the Great Awakening. He spent his last seven years in a small Indian outpost called Stockbridge, as a missionary to the Indians.

Many people still regard Edwards as America's leading philosopher and theologian. Countless theologians and evangelists testify to the importance of his writings. The English Baptist preacher C.H. Spurgeon wrote:

Did not Jonathan Edwards preach to sinners, and who more clear and explicit on these doctrinal matters? In the history of the church, with but few exceptions, you could not find a revival at all that was not produced by the orthodox faith. If you turn to the continent of America, how gross the falsehood that Calvinistic doctrine is unfavourable to revivals! Look at that wondrous shaking under Jonathan Edwards.[1]

B.B. Warfield was of the opinion that Edward's championing of Calvinism delayed the arrival of Arminianism in New England for a hundred years.

Dr Martyn Lloyd-Jones went so far as to say that 'no man is more relevant to the present condition of Christianity than Jonathan Edwards.'

During the 1980s, when the controversy over the work of the Holy Spirit in the life of local Christian fellowships was at its height, a book called *Delusion or Dynamite?* was published.[2] Clearly, it was intended to please everybody, as it had a Foreword by Michael Harper and an Afterword by Dr J.I. Packer. In an attempt to give readers some guidelines with which they could evaluate the work of the Holy Spirit and distinguish the genuine from the spurious, Dr Packer went back to the writings of Jonathan Edwards:

> The classic way of vindicating the authenticity of a spiritual movement, without denying reality to the follies and oddities criticized, is that of Jonathan Edwards. In his discussions of the Great Awakening he argues, first, that one should judge a movement not by its outward form, which may be bewildering, but by its abiding fruit; and, second, that any movement which (1) exalts Christ as divine Saviour, (2) opposes Satan's kingdom by weaning people from sin, (3) induces trust in the Bible as the word of God, (4) makes folk feel the urgency of eternal issues and their utter lostness without Christ, and (5) makes them love Christ and others, must be of God, whatever its disfigurements; for Satan and fallen mankind do not wish to see these effects, and try to avoid them. Those who know the facts will see this reasoning as settling the issue with regard to both the evangelical student movement and the charismatic renewal.

The present anthology of Jonathan Edwards's writings includes sections from his two most popular theological works: *The Distinguishing Marks of a Work of the Spirit of God. Applied to that*

Uncommon Operation that has Lately Appeared on the Minds of Many of the People of this Land, and *A Treatise Concerning Religious Affections.*

On 12 August, 1994, a headline appeared on the front page of the *Church Times* announcing 'Now they're dropping in Gloucestershire'. The story, by Betty Saunders, said:

> The Spirit which laid flat the packed congregations of two Evangelical strongholds in London (Holy Trinity, Brompton, and St Paul's, Onslow Square) is visiting the village church of St James, at Bream in Gloucestershire. For the past five weeks, when the Vicar, the Revd Alastair Kendall, has called down the power of the Holy Spirit, people have fallen to the floor, laughing, crying or speaking in tongues … The phenomenon struck HTB (Holy Trinity, Brompton) at a staff meeting. The wind of the Spirit is believed to have blown over from Canada, from the Airport Vineyard Church in Toronto.

An inside page of the same issue of the *Church Times* carried a report about the sixth annual New Wine worship and teaching holiday, under the heading 'Lots and lots of laughter' heard at a West Country worship holiday in which 'seminars full of people laughing and "going out" in the Holy Spirit' were among 'the main attractions'. Colin Moreton's report continued:

> The event has a distinct emphasis on 'ministering in the Spirit', and this year acted as something of a get-together for the members and leaders of those churches that have recently experienced a dramatic and well-publicized rise in charismatic activity. Among them was the Revd Sandy Millar, of Holy Trinity, Brompton, who spoke on how to handle church growth. He and the Rt Revd David Pytches, Vicar of St Andrew's Chorleywood, are among several British churchmen who have been to the USA and Canada to learn from the charismatic experience of the Vineyard churches there. This week crowds gath-

ered early for seminars in which Bishop Pytches sought to 'share the blessing' he had received at the Toronto Vineyard. The New Wine co-ordinator, Joyce Wills, said: 'A great many people have been touched by the Holy Spirit here. Some have been going out in the Spirit and having a wonderful, real experience of the presence of Jesus. There has been some exaggerated physical movement and lots and lots of laughter.'

In the opening pages of Edwards's *The Distinguishing Marks of a work of the Spirit of God* he writes: 'A work of God is not to be judged by any effects on the bodies of men; such as tears, trembling, groans, loud outcries, agonies of body, or the failure of bodily strength.' For anyone perplexed by recent reports about what claim to be new spiritual phenomena, Edwards's 'Nine Negative Signs' listed in his *Distinguishing Marks* make compulsive reading. One of the most interesting conclusions he comes to is that many of the 'abuses' which so often accompany revival situations in no way invalidate a true work of God's Holy Spirit.

Edwards also addressed the thorny subject of the place of 'affections', or emotions, in the Christian life in his book *A Treatise Concerning Religious Affections*. In it he tackles the question, 'What is the nature of true religion?' against the backdrop of the 1740–42 revival in America, which was being attacked scathingly by many prominent Christians.

The present collection of Edwards's writings is not confined to controversial topics. It includes his first published work, a sermon entitled 'God Glorified', and two other sermons, 'The Peace of Christ' and 'Christian Charity'. Edwards's preaching in 'Christian Charity' pre-empts the painful discussions some Christians engaged in during the 1970s and 1980s about the difference between the 'social gospel' and 'social implications and dimension of the gospel'. Edwards is not shy to declare that 'God has threatened uncharitable people, that if ever they come to be in calamity and distress they shall be left helpless: "Whoso stoppeth his ears at the cry of the poor, shall cry himself and not be heard" (Proverbs

21:3).' Edwards then proceeds to shoot down eleven objections 'which are sometimes made to the exercise of charity'.

While Edwards will always remain a controversial figure for some people, all are agreed that his overwhelming priority in all his writings was to be faithful to the teaching of the Bible, which he regarded as the Word of God. It is little wonder that George Whitefield wrote of Jonathan Edwards in his Journals, 'Mr Edwards is a solid, excellent Christian. I think I have not seen his fellow in all New England.' Concerning a controversial matter of the day, the Revd Israel Holly gave this advice to a friend:

> If I was to engage you in this controversy, I would say 'Read Edwards'. And if you wrote again, I would tell you 'Read Edwards'. For I think it needless for any man to write after him, and fruitless for any man to write against him upon this subject.[3]

Robert Backhouse
Norfolk 1995

References
1. C.H. Spurgeon, *Autobiography* vol.2: The Full Harvest, 1973, p.46.
2. Gervais Angel, *Delusion or Dynamite?: Reflections on a Quarter-Century of Charismatic Renewal*. Eastbourne: MARC, 1989.
3. Ola Winslow, *Historical Magazine*, 1867, p.234 (quoted by Iain H. Murray, *Jonathan Edwards: A New Biography*, Edinburgh: Banner of Truth, 1987. p.471).

God glorified in
man's dependence

That no flesh should glory in his presence. But of him are ye in Christ Jesus, who of God is made unto us wisdom, and righteousness, and sanctification, and redemption: that, according as it is written, He that glorieth, let him glory in the Lord. (1 Corinthians 1:29-31)

Those Christians to whom the apostle directed this epistle dwelt in a part of the world where human wisdom was in great repute; as the apostle observes in the twenty-second verse of this chapter, 'The Greeks seek after wisdom'. Corinth was not far from Athens, that had been for many ages the most famous seat of philosophy and learning in the world. The apostle therefore observes how God by the gospel destroyed, and brought to nought, their wisdom. The learned Greeks, and their great philosophers, by all their wisdom did not know God; they were not able to find out the truth in divine things. But, after they had done their utmost to no effect, it pleased God at length to reveal himself by the gospel, which they accounted foolishness. He 'chose the foolish things of the world to confound the wise, and the weak things of the world to confound the things which are mighty, and the base things of the world, and things that are despised, yea, and things which are not, to bring to nought the things that are.' And the apostle informs them why he did so – *That no flesh should glory in his presence.* In these words note the following:

God's aim

What God aims at in the way things are arranged in the matter of redemption is that man should not glory in himself, but only in God – *That no flesh should glory in his presence... that, according as it is written, He that glorieth, let him glory in the Lord.*

How this aim is attained

This end is attained in the work of redemption by that absolute and immediate dependence which men have upon God in that work, for all their good.

The good they have in and through Christ

He *is made unto us wisdom, righteousness, sanctification, and redemption.* All the good of the fallen and redeemed creature is concerned in these four things, and cannot be better distributed than into them; but Christ is each of them to us, and we have none of them in any other way than in him.

Wisdom: in him are all the proper good and true excellence of the understanding. Wisdom was a thing that the Greeks admired; but Christ is the true light of the world; it is through him alone that true wisdom is imparted to the mind.

Righteousness: it is by being in Christ that we are justified, have our sins pardoned, and are received as righteous into God's favour.

Sanctification: in Christ we have true excellence of heart as well as of understanding; and he is made unto us inherent as well as imputed righteousness.

Redemption: it is by Christ that we have the actual deliverance from all misery, and the gift of all happiness and glory.

Thus we have all our good by Christ, who is God.

It is God that has given us Christ

Another instance in which appears our dependence on God for all our good is that it is God who has given us Christ, that we might have these benefits through him.

2

God gives us faith

It is of him that we are in Christ Jesus, and come to have an interest in him, and so receive those blessings which he is made unto us. It is God that gives us faith whereby we close with Christ.

So this verse shows our dependence on each person in the Trinity for all our good. We are dependent on Christ the Son of God, as he is our wisdom, righteousness, sanctification, and redemption. We are dependent on the Father, who has given us Christ, and made him to be these things to us. We are dependent on the Holy Spirit, for it is *of him that we are in Christ Jesus;* it is the Spirit of God that gives faith in him, whereby we receive him, and close with him.

Doctrine

'God is glorified in the work of redemption in this, that there appears in it so absolute and universal a dependence of the redeemed on him.'

Absolute and universal dependence

There is an absolute and universal dependence of the redeemed on God for all their good. The nature and contrivance of our redemption is such that the redeemed are in everything directly, immediately, and entirely dependent on God: they are dependent on him for all, and are dependent on him in every way. The various ways in which one being may be dependent on another for its good, and in which those redeemed by Jesus Christ depend on God for all their good, are these: he is the *cause* and original from which all their good comes – it is *of* him; and he is the *medium* by which it is obtained and conveyed – they have it *through* him; and he is the *good* itself – it is *in* him. In all these respects, those who are redeemed by Jesus Christ depend very directly and entirely on God for their all.

3

God is the great *author* of it. He is the *first* cause of it; and not only that, but he is the *only* proper cause. It is of God that we have our Redeemer. It is God that has provided a Saviour for us. Jesus Christ is not only of God in his person, as he is the only-begotten Son of God, but he is from God, as we are concerned in him, and in his office of Mediator. He is the gift of God to us: God chose and anointed him, appointed him his work, and sent him into the world. And as it is God that *gives*, so it is God that *accepts* the Saviour. He gives the purchaser, and he affords the thing purchased.

It is of God that Christ becomes ours, that we are brought to him, and are united to him. It is of God that we receive faith to close with him, that we may have an interest in him. 'For by grace are ye saved, through faith; and that not of yourselves, it is the gift of God' (Ephesians 2:8). It is of God that we actually receive all the benefits that Christ has purchased. It is God that pardons and justifies, and delivers from going down to hell; and into his favour the redeemed are received, when they are justified. So it is God that delivers from the dominion of sin, cleanses us from our filthiness, and changes us from our deformity. It is of God that the redeemed receive all their true excellence, wisdom, and holiness; and that in two ways, namely, as the Holy Spirit by whom these things are immediately wrought is from God, proceeds from him, and is sent by him; and also as the Holy Spirit himself is God, by whose operation and indwelling the knowledge of God and divine things, a holy disposition and all grace, are conferred and upheld. And though means are made use of in conferring grace on men's souls, yet it is of God that we have these means of grace, and it is he that makes them effectual. It is of God that we have the Holy Scriptures; they are his word. It is of God that we have ordinances, and their efficacy depends on the immediate influence of his Spirit. The ministers of the gospel are sent of God, and all their suffi-ciency is of him 'We have this treasure in earthen vessels, that the excellency of the power may be of God, and not of us' (2

4

Corinthians 4:7). Their success depends entirely and absolutely on the immediate blessing and influence of God.

Grace: The redeemed have all from the grace of God. It was of mere grace that God gave us his only-begotten Son. The grace is great in proportion to the excellence of what is given. The gift was infinitely precious, because it was of a person infinitely worthy, a person of infinite glory; and also because it was of a person infinitely near and dear to God. The grace is great in proportion to the benefit we have given us in him. The benefit is doubly infinite, in that in him we have deliverance from an infinite, because an eternal, misery, and do also receive eternal joy and glory. The grace in bestowing this gift is great in proportion to our unworthiness to whom it is given; instead of deserving such a gift, we merited infinitely ill of God's hands. The grace is great according to the manner of giving, or in proportion to the humiliation and expense of the method and means by which a way is made for our having the gift. He gave him to dwell amongst us; he gave him to us incarnate, or in our nature; and in similar though sinless infirmities. He gave him to us in a low and afflicted state; and not only so, but as slain, that he might be a feast for our souls.

The grace of God in bestowing this gift is most free. It was what God was under no obligation to bestow. He might have rejected fallen man, as he did the fallen angels. It was what we never did anything to merit; it was given while we were still enemies, and before we had so much as repented. It was from the love of God who saw no excellence in us to attract it; and it was without expectation of ever being requited for it. And it is from mere grace that the benefits of Christ are applied to such and such particular persons. Those that are called and sanctified are to attribute it solely to the good pleasure of God's goodness, by which they are distinguished. He is sovereign, and has mercy on whom he will have mercy.

Man has now a greater dependence on the grace of God than he had before the fall. He depends on the free goodness of God for much more than he did then. Then he depended on God's goodness for conferring the reward of the perfect obedience; for God was not obliged to promise and bestow that reward. But now we are dependent on the grace of God for much more; we stand in need of grace, not only to bestow glory upon us, but to deliver us from hell and eternal wrath. Under the first covenant we depended on God's goodness to give us the reward of righteousness; and so we do now: but we stand in need of God's free and sovereign grace to give us that righteousness; to pardon our sin, and release us from the guilt and infinite demerit of it.

And as we are dependent on the goodness of God for more now than under the first covenant, so we are dependent on much greater, more free and wonderful goodness. We are no more dependent on God's arbitrary and sovereign good pleasure. In our first state we were dependent on God for holiness. We had our original righteousness from him; but then holiness was not bestowed in such a way of sovereign good pleasure as it is now. Man was created holy, for it became God to create holy all his rational creatures. It would have been a disparagement to the holiness of God's nature if he had made an intelligent creature unholy. But now when fallen man is made holy, it is from mere and arbitrary grace; God may for ever deny holiness to the fallen creature if he pleases, without any disparagement to any of his perfections.

And we are not only indeed more dependent on the grace of God, but our dependence is much more conspicuous, because our own insufficiency and helplessness in ourselves is much more apparent in our fallen and undone state, than it was before we were either sinful or miserable. We are more obviously dependent on God for holiness, because we are first sinful, and utterly polluted, and afterwards holy. So the production of the effect is tangible, and its derivation from God more obvious. If man was ever holy and always so, it would not be so apparent that he did not have holiness necessarily, as an inseparable qualification of human nature. So we are more clearly dependent on free grace for the favour of God, for we are first justly the objects of his displeasure, and afterwards are received into favour. We are more clearly dependent on God for happiness, being first miserable, and afterwards happy. It is more obviously free and without merit in us, because we are actually without any kind of excellence to merit, if there could be any such thing as merit in creature-excellency. And we are not only without any true excellence, but are full of, and wholly defiled with, that which is infinitely odious. All our good is more obviously from God because we are first naked and wholly without any good, and afterwards enriched with all good.

Power: We receive all from the power of God. Man's redemption is often spoken of as a work of wonderful power as well as grace. The great power of God appears in bringing a sinner from his low state, from the depths of sin and misery, to such an exalted state of holiness and happiness. 'And what is the exceeding greatness of his power to us-ward who believe, according to the working of his mighty power' (Ephesians 1:19).

We are dependent on God's power through every step of our redemption. We are dependent on the power of God to convert us, and give faith in Jesus Christ, and the new nature. It is a work of creation: 'If any man be in Christ, he is a new creature' (2 Corinthians 5:17). 'We are created in Christ Jesus' (Ephesians 2:10). The fallen creature cannot attain to true holiness, except by being created again. 'And that ye put on the new man, which after God is created in righteousness and true holiness' (Ephesians 4:24). It is a raising from the dead. 'Wherein also ye are risen with him through the faith of the operation of God, who hath raised him from the dead' (Colossians 2:12-13). It is a more glorious work of power than mere creation, or raising a dead body to life, in that the effect attained is greater and more excellent. That holy and happy being, and spiritual life, which is produced in the work of conversion, is a far greater and more glorious effect than mere being and life. And the state from which the change is made – a death in sin, a total corruption of nature, and depth of misery – is far more remote from the state attained than mere death or non-entity.

It is by God's power also that we are preserved in a state of grace. 'Who are kept by the power of God through faith unto salvation' (1 Peter 1:5). As grace is at first from God, so it is continually from him, and is maintained by him, as much as light in the atmosphere is all day long from the sun, as well as at first dawning, or sunrising. Men are dependent on the power of God for every exercise of grace, and for carrying on that work in the heart, for subduing sin and corruption, increasing holy principles, and enabling to bring forth fruit in good works. Man is dependent on divine power in bringing grace to its perfection, in making the soul completely amiable in Christ's glorious likeness, and filling it with a satisfying joy and blessedness; and for the raising of the body to life, and to such a perfect state, that it shall be suitable for a habitation and organ for a soul so perfected and blessed. These are the most glorious effects of the power of God, that are seen in the series of God's acts with respect to the creatures.

Man was dependent on the power of God in his first state, but he is more dependent on his power now; he needs God's power to do more things for him, and depends on a more wonderful exercise of his power. It was an effect of the power of God to make man holy at the first; not more remarkably so now, because there is a great deal of opposition and difficulty in the way. It is a more glorious effect of power to make holy what was so depraved, and under the dominion of sin, than to confer holiness on what had nothing contrary before. It is a more glorious work of power to rescue a soul out of the hands of the devil, and from the powers of darkness, and to bring it into a state of salvation, than to confer holiness where there was no prepossession or opposition. 'When a strong man armed keepeth his palace, his goods are in peace; but when a stronger than he shall come upon him, and overcome him, he taketh from him all his armour, wherein he trusted, and divideth his spoils' (Luke 11:21-22). So it is a more glorious work of power to uphold a soul in a state of grace and holiness, and to carry it on till it is brought to glory, when there is so much sin remaining in the heart resisting, and Satan with all his might opposing, than it would have been to have kept man from falling at first, when Satan had nothing in man.

Thus we have shown how the redeemed are dependent on God for all their good, as they have all of him.

God is the medium of it, as well as the author and fountain of it. All we have wisdom, the pardon of sin, deliverance from hell, acceptance into God's favour, grace and holiness, true comfort and happiness, eternal life and glory, is from God by a Mediator; and this Mediator is God; which Mediator we have an absolute dependence upon, as he through whom we receive all. So here is another way in which we have our dependence on God for all good. God not only gives us the Mediator, and accepts his mediation, and of his power and grace bestows the things purchased by the Mediator; but he the Mediator is God.

Our blessings are what we have by purchase; and the purchase is made of God, the blessings are purchased of him, and God gives the purchaser; and not only so, but God is the purchaser. God is both the purchaser and the price; for Christ, who is God, purchased these blessings for us, by offering up himself as the price of our salvation. He purchased eternal life by the sacrifice of himself. 'He offered up himself' (Hebrews 7:27). 'He hath appeared to take away sin by the sacrifice of himself' (Hebrews 9:26). Indeed it was the human nature that was offered; but it was the same person with the divine, and therefore was an infinite price.

As we thus have our good through God, we have a dependence on him in a respect that man in his first state did not have. Man was to have eternal life then through his own righteousness, so he was partly dependent on what was in himself; for we are dependent on that through which we have our good, as well as that from which we have it: and though man's righteousness that he then depended on was indeed from God, yet it was his own, it was inherent in himself; so his dependence was not so immediately on God. But now the righteousness that we are dependent on is not in ourselves, but in God. We are saved through the righteousness of Christ. He is *made unto us righteousness,* and therefore is prophesied under the name of 'the Lord our righteousness' (Jeremiah 23:6). In that the righteousness we are justified by is the righteousness of Christ, it is the righteousness of God.

'That we might be made the righteousness of God in him' (2 Corinthians 5:21). Thus in redemption we have not only all things of God, but by and through him. 'But to us there is but one God, the Father, of whom are all things, and we in him; and one Lord Jesus Christ, by whom are all things, and we by him' (1 Corinthians 8:6).

They have it in God

We not only have all our good of him, and through him, but it consists in him; he is all our good. The good of the redeemed is either objective or inherent. By their objective good, I mean that extrinsic object, in the possession and enjoyment of which they are happy. Their inherent good is that excellency or pleasure which is in the soul itself. With respect to both of these, the redeemed have all their good in God, or (which is the same thing) God himself is all their good.

Objective good: God himself is the great good which the redeemed are brought to possess and enjoy by redemption. He is the highest good, and the sum of all that good which Christ purchased. God is the inheritance of the saints; he is the portion of their souls. God is their wealth and treasure, their food, their life, their dwelling-place, their ornament and diadem, and their everlasting honour and glory. They have none in heaven but God; he is the great good which the redeemed are received to at death, and which they are to rise to at the end of the world. The Lord God is the light of the heavenly Jerusalem; and is the 'river of the water of life' that runs, and 'the tree of life that grows, in the midst of the paradise of God.' The glorious excellencies and beauty of God will be what will for ever entertain the minds of the saints, and the love of God will be their everlasting feast. The redeemed will indeed enjoy other things; they will enjoy the angels, and will enjoy one another; but that which they shall enjoy in the angels, or each others, or in anything else whatsoever that will yield them delight and happiness, will be what is seen of God in them.

Inherent good: Inherent good is twofold: it is either excellence or pleasure. These the redeemed not only derive from God, as caused

10

by him, but have them in him. They have spiritual excellence and joy by a kind of participation of God. They are made excellent by a communication of God's excellence. God puts his own beauty, i.e. his beautiful likeness, upon their souls. They are made partakers of the divine nature, or moral image of God (2 Peter 1:4). They are holy by being made partakers of God's holiness (Hebrews 12:10). The saints are beautiful and blessed by a communication of God's holiness and joy, as the moon and planets are bright by the sun's light. The saint has spiritual joy and pleasure by a kind of effusion of God on the soul. In these things the redeemed have communion with God; that is, they partake with him and of him.

The saints have both their spiritual excellence and blessedness by the gift of the Holy Spirit, and his dwelling in them. They are not only caused by the Holy Spirit, but are in him as their principle. The Holy Spirit becoming an inhabitant is a vital principle in the soul. He, acting in, upon, and with the soul, becomes a fountain of true holiness and joy, like a spring of water. 'But whosoever drinketh of the water that I shall give him, shall never thirst; but the water that I shall give him, shall be in him a well of water springing up into everlasting life' (John 4:14). 'He that believeth on me, as the Scripture hath said, out of his belly shall flow rivers of living water; but this spake he of the Spirit, which they that believe on him should receive' (John 7:38–39). The sum of what Christ has purchased for us is that spring of water spoken of in the first of these passages, and those rivers of living water spoken of in the second. And the sum of the blessings which the redeemed will receive in heaven, is that river of water of life that proceeds from the throne of God and the Lamb (Revelation 22:1). Doubtless this signifies the same as those rivers of living water in John 7:38–39, which is elsewhere called the 'river of God's pleasures'. In this consists the fullness of good which the saints receive of Christ. It is by partaking of the Holy Spirit that they have communion with Christ in his fullness. God has given him the Spirit without limit; they receive of his fullness, and grace for grace. This is the sum of the saints' inheritance; and therefore that little of the Holy Spirit which believers have in this world is said to be the earnest of their inheritance: 'Who hath also sealed us, and given us the Spirit in our hearts' (2 Corinthians 1:22). 'Now he that hath wrought us for the self same thing, is God, who also hath given unto us the earnest of the Spirit' (2 Corinthians 5:5). 'Ye were sealed with that holy Spirit of promise, which is the earnest of our inheritance, until the redemption of the purchased possession' (Ephesians 1:13-14).

The Holy Spirit and good things are spoken of in Scripture as the same, as if the Spirit of God communicated to the soul, comprised all good things. 'How much more shall your heavenly Father give good things to them that ask him?' (Matthew 7:11). In Luke it is, 'How much more shall your heavenly Father give the Holy Spirit to them that ask him!' (Luke 11:13). This is the sum of the blessings that Christ died to procure, and the subject of gospel promises. 'He was made a curse for us, that we might receive the promise of the Spirit through faith' (Galatians 3:13-14). The Spirit of God is the great promise of the Father: 'Behold, I send the promise of my Father upon you' (Luke 24:49). The Spirit is God therefore is called 'the Spirit of promise' (Ephesians 1:33). This promised thing Christ received, and had given into his hand, as soon as he had finished the work of our redemption, to bestow on all that he had redeemed: 'Therefore being by the right hand of God exalted, and having received of the Father the promise of the Holy Ghost, he hath shed forth this, which ye both see and hear' (Acts 2:13). So all the holiness and happiness of the redeemed is in God. It is in the communications, indwelling, and acting of the Spirit of God. Holiness and happiness is in the fruit, here and hereafter, because God dwells in them, and they in God.

Thus God has given us the Redeemer, and it is by him that our good is purchased. So God is the Redeemer and the price; and he also is the good purchased. So all that we have is of God, and through him, and in him. 'For of him, and through him, and to him, or in him, are all things' (Romans 11:36). The same Greek words that are here rendered *to him* are in 1 Corinthians 8:6 rendered *in him*.

God is glorified

God is glorified in the work of redemption by this means – by there being so great and universal a dependence of the redeemed on him.

A reason to acknowledge God's perfections

Man has so much the greater occasion and obligation to notice and acknowledge God's perfections and all-sufficiency. The greater the creature's dependence is on God's perfections, and the greater concern he has with them, so much the greater occasion has he to take notice of them. The more his concern with God's power and grace, and dependence on it, the more reason he has to take notice of that power and grace. The greater and more immediate his dependence on the divine goodness, the more reason there is to take notice of and acknowledge that. The greater and more absolute our dependence on the divine perfections, as belonging to the different persons of the Trinity, the more occasion we have to observe and own the divine glory of each of them. What we are most concerned with is surely most in the way of our observation and notice; and this kind of concern with anything, this dependence, tends especially to command and oblige the attention and observation. It is easy to neglect things that we are not much dependent upon, but we can scarce do anything but mind that which we have a great dependence on.

By reason of our so great dependence on God, and his perfections, and in so many respects, he and his glory are the more directly set in our view, whichever way we turn our eyes.

We have the greater occasion to take notice of God's all-sufficiency, when all our sufficiency is thus of him in every way. We have the more occasion to contemplate him as an infinite good, and as the fountain of all good. Such a dependence on God demonstrates his all-sufficiency. So much the greater does the creature's emptiness in himself appear; and so much the greater the creature's emptiness, so much the greater must the fullness of the Being be who supplies him. Our having all *of* God shows the fullness of his power and grace; our having all *through* him shows the fullness of his merit and worthiness; and our having all *in* him demonstrates his fullness of beauty, love, and happiness. And the redeemed, by reason of the greatness of their dependence on God, have not only so much the greater occasion, but obligation to contemplate and acknowledge the glory and fullness of God. How unreasonable and ungrateful should we be if we did not acknowledge that sufficiency and glory which we absolutely, immediately, and universally depend upon!

God's great glory compared with the creature's

Because the creature is thus wholly and universally dependent on God, it is apparent that the creature is nothing, and that God is all. Thus we see that God is infinitely above us – that God's strength, wisdom, and holiness are infinitely greater than ours. However great and glorious the creature sees God to be, if he is not aware of the difference between God and him, so as to see that God's glory is great compared with his own, he will not be disposed to give God the glory due to his name. If the creature in any respects sets himself on a level with God, or exalts himself to any competition with him, however he may apprehend that great honour and profound respect may belong to God from those that are at a greater distance, he will not be so conscious of its being due from him. The more men exalt themselves, the less will they surely be disposed to exalt God. It is certainly what God aims at in the disposition of things in redemption (if we allow the Scriptures to be a revelation of God's mind) that God should appear full, and man in himself empty, that God should appear all, and man nothing. It is God's declared intention that others should not 'glory in his presence'; which implies that it is his intention to advance his own comparative glory. The more man 'glories in God's presence', the less glory is ascribed to God.

Creatures to be wholly given to God

Because the creature depends on God so absolutely and universally, provision is made that God should have our whole souls, and should

14

be the object of our undivided respect. If we were partly dependent on God, and partly on something else, man's respect would be divided. Thus it would be if we depended on God only for a part of our good, and on ourselves, or some other being, for another part – or if we had our good only from God, and through another that was not God, and in something else distinct from both, our hearts would be divided between the good itself, and him from whom, and him through whom, we received it. But now there is no occasion for this, God being not only he from whom we have all good, but also through whom, and is that good itself, that we have from him and through him. Whatever there is to attract our respect, the tendency is still directly towards God. All unites in him as the centre.

Use

God's marvellous wisdom in the work of redemption

God has made man's emptiness and misery, his low, lost, and ruined state, into which he sank by the fall, an occasion of the greater advancement of his own glory – particularly in that there is now much more universal and apparent dependence of man on God. God is pleased to lift man out of that dismal abyss of sin and woe into which he had fallen, and exceedingly to exalt him in excellence and honour, yet the creature has nothing to glory of in any respect; all the glory evidently belongs to God, all is in a mere, and most absolute and divine, dependence on the Father, Son, and Holy Spirit. And each person of the Trinity is equally glorified in this work; there is an absolute dependence of the creature on every one for all: all is of the Father, all through the Son, and all in the Holy Spirit. Thus God appears in the work of redemption as all in all. It is fit that he who is, and there is none else, should be the Alpha and Omega, the first and the last, the all and the only, in this work.

Hence those doctrines and schemes of divinity that are in any respect opposite to such an absolute and universal dependence on God derogate from his glory, and thwart the purpose of our redemption. And such are those schemes that put the creature in God's stead, in any of the respects mentioned, that exalt man into the place of either Father, Son, or Holy Spirit, in anything pertaining to our redemption. However they may allow of a dependence of the redeemed on God, they still deny a dependence that is so *absolute* and universal. They own an entire dependence on God for *some* things, but not for others; they own that we depend on God for the gift and acceptance of a Redeemer, but deny so absolute a dependence on him for obtaining an *interest* in the Redeemer. They own an absolute dependence on the Father for giving his Son, and on the Son for working our redemption, but not so entire a dependence on the Holy Spirit for *conversion*, and for being in Christ, and so becoming entitled to his benefits. They own a dependence on God for *means* of grace, but not absolutely for the benefits and success of those means; a partial dependence on the power of God, for obtaining and exercising holiness, but not a mere dependence on the arbitrary and sovereign grace of God. They own a dependence on the free grace of God for receiving us into his favour, without any merit of our own, but not as it is without being attracted, or moved with any excellence. They own a partial dependence on Christ, as he through whom we have life, as having purchased new terms of life, but still hold that the righteousness through which we have life is inherent in ourselves, as it was under the first covenant. Now whatever scheme is inconsistent with our *entire* dependence on God for all, and of having all of him, through him, and in him, it is repugnant to the purpose and tenor of the gospel, and robs it of that which God accounts its lustre and glory.

Why it is by faith that we come to have an interest in redemption

The nature of faith includes a conscious acknowledgement of *absolute dependence* on God in this matter. It is very fit that in order to have the benefit of this redemption, everyone should be required to be aware of, and acknowledge, their dependence on God for it. By this means God has contrived to glorify himself in redemption; and it is fit that he should at least have this glory of those that are the subjects of this redemption, and have the benefit of it.

Faith is being conscious of what is real in the work of redemption; and the soul that believes depends on God entirely for all salvation, in its own sense and act. Faith abases men, and exalts God; it gives all the glory of redemption to him alone. Saving faith requires man to be emptied of himself, to be aware that he is 'wretched, and miserable, and poor, and blind, and naked'. Humility is a great ingredient of true faith: he that truly receives redemption receives it as a little child. 'Whosoever shall not receive the kingdom of heaven as a little child, he shall not enter therein' (Mark 10:15). It is the delight of a believing soul to abuse itself and exalt God alone: that is the language of it – 'Not unto us, O Lord, not unto us, but to thy name give glory' (Psalm 115:1).

Exalt God alone

Let us ascribe to God all the glory of redemption. Let us endeavour to obtain, and increase in, an awareness of our great dependence on God, to have our eye on him alone, to mortify a self-dependent and self-righteous disposition. Man is naturally exceedingly prone to exalt himself, and depend on his own power or goodness, as though he must expect happiness from himself. He is prone to have respect to enjoyments alien from God and his Spirit, as those in which happiness is to be found. But this doctrine should teach us to exalt God *alone* – by trust and reliance, but also by praise. *Let him that glorieth, glory in the Lord.* Does anyone hope that he is converted, and sanctified, and that his mind is endowed with true

17

excellence and spiritual beauty? Does anyone hope that his sins are forgiven, and that he is received into God's favour, and exalted to the honour and blessedness of being his child, and an heir of eternal life? Let him give all the glory to God, who alone makes him different from the worst of men in this world, or the most miserable of the damned in hell. Does anyone have comfort and strong hope of eternal life? Let not his hope lift him up, but rather dispose him to abase himself all the more, to reflect on his own exceeding unworthiness of such a favour, and to exalt God alone. Is anyone eminent in holiness, and abundant in good works? Let him take nothing of the glory of it to himself, but ascribe it to him whose 'workmanship we are, created in Christ Jesus unto good works' (Ephesians 2:10).

The distinguishing marks of
a work of the Spirit of God:
Part 1

Beloved, believe not every spirit, but try the spirits whether they are of God: because many false prophets are gone out into the world. (1 John 4:1)

In the apostolic age, there was the greatest outpouring of the Spirit of God that ever was, both as to his extraordinary influences and gifts, and his ordinary operations, in convincing, converting, enlightening, and sanctifying the souls of men. But as the influences of the true Spirit abounded, so counterfeits did also abound: the devil was abundant in mimicking, both the ordinary and extraordinary influences of the Spirit of God, as is manifest by innumerable passages of the apostles' writings. This made it very necessary that the church of Christ should be furnished with some certain rules, distinguishing and clear marks, by which she might proceed safely in judging of the true from the false without danger of being imposed upon. The giving of such rules is the plain design of this chapter, where we have this matter more expressly and fully treated of than anywhere else in the Bible. The apostle, of set purpose, undertakes to supply the church of God with such marks of the true Spirit as may be plain and safe, and well accommodated to use and practice; and that the subject might be clearly and sufficiently handled, he insists upon it throughout the chapter, which makes it wonderful that what is said here is no more taken notice of in this extraordinary day, when there is such an uncommon and extensive operation on the minds of people, such a variety of opinions concerning it, and so much talk about the work of the Spirit.

The apostle's discourse on this subject is introduced by an occasional mention of the indwelling of the Spirit, as the sure evidence of an interest in Christ. 'And he that keepeth his commandments dwelleth in him, and he in him; and hereby we know that he abideth in us, by the Spirit which he hath given us.' From this we may infer that the apostle's purpose is not only to give marks by which to distinguish the true Spirit from the false, in his extraordinary gifts of prophecy and miracles, but also in his ordinary influences on the minds of his people, in order that they may be united to Christ, and be built up in him. This is also manifest from the marks themselves that are given, which we shall consider later.

The words of the text are an introduction to this discourse of the distinguishing signs of the true and false Spirit. Before the apostle proceeds to lay down these signs, he exhorts Christians, first, against being over-credulous, and forward to admit every specious appearance as a work of a true Spirit. 'Beloved, believe not every spirit, but try the spirits whether they are of God.' And, second, he shows that there were many counterfeits, 'because many false prophets are gone out into the world'. These not only claimed to have the Spirit of God in his extraordinary gifts of inspiration, but also to be the great friends and favourites of heaven, to be eminently holy persons, and to have much of the ordinary saving, sanctifying influences of the Spirit of God on their hearts. Hence we are to look upon these words as a direction to examine and try their claims to the Spirit of God in both these respects.

My purpose therefore at this time is to show what are the true, certain, and distinguishing evidences of a work of the Spirit of God, by which we may safely proceed in judging any operation we find in ourselves, or see in others. And here I would observe that we are to take the *Scriptures* as our guide in such cases. This is the great and standing rule which God has given to his church, in order to guide them in things relating to the great concerns of their souls; and it is an infallible and sufficient rule. There are undoubtedly sufficient marks given to guide the church of God in this great affair of judging of spirits, without which it would lie open to woeful delusion, and would be remedilessly exposed to be imposed on and devoured by its enemies. And we need not be afraid to trust these rules. Doubtless that Spirit who indited the Scriptures knew how to give us good rules, by which to distinguish his operations from all that is falsely claimed to be from him. And this, as I observed before, the Spirit of God has here done of set purpose, and done it more particularly and fully than anywhere else; so that in my present discourse I shall go nowhere else for rules or marks for the trial of spirits, but shall confine myself to those that I find in this chapter.

But before I proceed to speak about these particularly, I would prepare my way by first observing *negatively,* in some instances, what are *not* signs or evidences of a work of the Spirit of God.

Negative signs

The unusual and extraordinary character of a work

Nothing can be certainly concluded from a work being carried on in a very unusual and extraordinary way, provided the variety or difference is such as may still be included within the limits of scriptural rules. What the church has been used to is not a rule by which we are to judge, because there may be new and extraordinary works of God, and he has hitherto evidently worked in an extraordinary manner. He has brought to pass new things, strange works; and has worked in such a manner as to surprise both men and angels. And as God has done thus in times past, so we have no reason to think but that he will still do so. The prophecies of Scripture give us reason to think that God has things to accomplish which have never yet been seen. No deviation from what has hitherto been usual, let it be never so great, is an argument that a work is not from the Spirit of God, if it is no deviation from his prescribed rule. The

Holy Spirit is sovereign in his operation; and we know that he uses a great variety; and we cannot tell how great a variety he may use, within the compass of the rules he himself has fixed. We ought not to limit God where he has not limited himself.

Therefore it is not reasonable to determine that a work is not from God's Holy Spirit because of the extraordinary degree in which the minds of persons are influenced. If they seem to have an extraordinary conviction of the dreadful nature of sin, and a very uncommon sense of the misery of a Christless condition – or extraordinary views of the certainty and glory of divine things – and are proportionably moved with very extraordinary affections of fear and sorrow, desire, love, or joy; or if the apparent change is very sudden, and the work carried on with very unusual swiftness – and the persons affected are very numerous, and many of them are very young, with other unusual circumstances, not infringing upon scriptural marks of a work of the Spirit – these things are no argument that the work is not of the Spirit of God. The extraordinary and unusual degree of influence, and power of operation, if in its nature it fits the rules and marks given in Scripture, is rather an argument in its favour; for by how much higher the degree which in its nature is agreeable to the rule, so much the more is there of conformity to the rule; and so much the more evident that conformity. When things are in small degrees, though they may really follow the rule, it is not so easily seen whether their nature agrees with the rule.

People are very apt to have doubts about things that are strange; especially elderly persons, who doubt that things are right which they have never been used to in their day, and have not heard of in the days of their fathers. But if it is a good argument that a work is not from the Spirit of God if it is very unusual, then it was so in the apostles' days. The work of the Spirit then was carried on in a manner that, in very many respects, was altogether new – such as had never been seen or heard since the world stood. The work was then carried on with more visible and remarkable power than ever; nor had there been seen before such mighty and wonderful effects of the Spirit of God in sudden changes and such great engagedness and zeal in great multitudes – such a sudden alteration in towns, cities, and countries; such a swift progress, and vast extent of the work – and many other extraordinary circumstances might be mentioned. The great unusualness of the work surprised the Jews; they knew not what to make of it, but could not believe it to be the work of God; many looked upon the persons that were the subjects of it as bereft of reason; as you may see in Acts 2:13 and 26:24, and in 1 Corinthians 4:10.

And we have reason from Scripture prophecy to suppose that at the commencement of the last and greatest outpouring of the Spirit of God that is to come in the latter ages of the world, the manner of the work will be very extraordinary, and such as has never yet been seen; so that there shall be occasion to say, as in Isaiah 56:8, 'Who hath heard such a thing? Who hath seen such things? Shall the earth be made to bring forth in one day? Shall a nation be born at once? for as soon as Zion travailed, she brought forth her children.' It may be reasonably expected that the extraordinary manner of the work then will bear some proportion to the very extraordinary events, and that glorious change in the state of the world, which God will bring to pass by it.

Bodily effects

A work is not to be judged of by any effects on the bodies of men, such as tears, trembling, groans, loud outcries, agonies of body, or the failing of bodily strength. The influence persons are under is not to be judged of one way or the other by such effects on the body; and the reason is, because the Scripture nowhere gives us any such rule. We cannot conclude that persons are under the influence of the Spirit because we see such effects upon their bodies, because this is not given as a mark of the true Spirit; nor on the other hand have we any reason to conclude from any such outward appearances that persons are not under the influence of the Spirit of God, because there is no rule of Scripture given us to judge of spirits by, that does either expressly or indirectly exclude such effects on the body, nor does reason exclude them. It is easily accounted for from the consideration of the nature of divine and eternal things, and the nature of man, and the laws of the union between soul and body, how a right influence, a true and proper sense of things, should have such effects on the body, even those that are of the most extraordinary kind, such as taking away the bodily strength, or throwing the body into great agonies, and extorting loud outcries. None of us does not suppose that the misery of hell is doubtless so dreadful, and eternity so vast, that if a person should have a clear apprehension of that misery as it is, it would be more than his feeble frame could bear, and especially if at the same time he saw himself in great danger of it, and to be utterly uncertain whether he would be delivered from it, and have no security from it one day or hour. If we consider human nature, we must not wonder that when persons have a great sense of that which is so amazingly dreadful, and also have a great view of their own wickedness and God's anger, that things seem to them to forebode speedy and immediate destruction. We see the nature of man to be such that when he is in danger of some terrible calamity to which he is greatly exposed, he is ready upon every occasion to think that it is coming *now*.

When people's hearts are full of fear, in time of war, they are ready to tremble at the shaking of a leaf, and to expect the enemy every minute, and to say within themselves, '*Now* I shall be slain.' If we should suppose that a person saw himself hanging over a great pit, full of fierce and glowing flames, by a thread that he knew to be very weak, and not sufficient to bear his weight, and knew that multitudes had been in such circumstances before, and that most of them had fallen and perished, and saw nothing within reach that he could take hold of to save him, what distress would he be in! How ready to think that *now* the thread was breaking, that now, *this minute,* he would be swallowed up in those dreadful flames! And would he not be ready to cry out in such circumstances? How much more those that see themselves in this manner hanging over an infinitely more dreadful pit, or held over it in the hand of God, who at the same time they see to be exceedingly provoked! No wonder that the wrath of God, when manifested only a little to the soul, over-bears human strength.

So it may easily be accounted for, that a true sense of the glorious excellence of the Lord Jesus Christ, and of his wonderful dying, love, and the exercise of a truly spiritual love and joy, should be such as very much to overcome the bodily strength. We are all ready to admit that no one can see God and live, and that it is only a very small part of that apprehension of the glory and love of Christ, which the saints enjoy in heaven, that our present frame can bear; therefore it is not at all strange that God should sometimes give his saints such foretastes of heaven as to diminish their bodily strength. If it was not unaccountable that the queen of Sheba fainted, and had her bodily strength taken away, when she came to see the glory of Solomon, much less is it unaccountable that she who is the antitype of the queen of Sheba – namely, the Church, that is brought, as it were, from the utmost ends of the earth, from being an alien and stranger, far off, in a state of sin and misery – should faint when she comes to see the glory of Christ, who is the antitype of Solomon; and especially will be so in that prosperous, peaceful, glorious kingdom, which he will set up in the world in its latter age.

Some people object against such extraordinary appearances, that we have no instances of them recorded in the New Testament, under the extraordinary effusions of the Spirit. Were this allowed, I can see no force in the objection, if neither reason nor any rule of Scripture exclude such things – especially considering what was observed under the last heading. I do not know that we have any express mention in the New Testament of any person's weeping, or groaning, or sighing through fear of hell, or a sense of God's anger; but is there anybody so foolish as to argue from this, that anyone in whom these things appear is not being convicted by the Spirit of God? And the reason why we do not argue thus is because these are easily accounted for from what we know of the nature of man, and from what the Scripture informs us in general concerning the nature of eternal things, and the nature of convictions of God's Spirit; so that there is no need that anything should be said in particular concerning these external, circumstantial effects. Nobody supposes that there is any need of express scripture for every external, accidental manifestation of the inward motion of the mind: and though such circumstances are not particularly recorded in sacred history, there is a great deal of reason to think, from the general accounts we have, that it could not be otherwise than that such things must be in those days.

And there is also reason to think that such great outpouring of the Spirit was not wholly without those more extraordinary effects on people's bodies. The jailer in particular seems to have been an instance of that nature, when he, in the utmost distress and amazement, came trembling, and fell down before Paul and Silas. His falling down at that time does not seem to be intentionally putting himself into a posture of supplication, or humble address to Paul and Silas; for he seems not to have said anything to them then; but he first brought them out, and then he says to them, 'Sirs, what must I do to be saved?' (Acts 16:29-30). But his falling down seems to be from the same cause as his trembling.

The psalmist gives an account of his crying out aloud, and a great weakening of his body under convictions of conscience, and a sense of the guilt of sin: 'When I kept silence my bones waxed old, through my roaring all the day long; for day and night thy hand was heavy upon me: my moisture is turned into the drought of summer' (Psalm 32:3-4). We may at least argue so much from it, that such an effect of conviction of sin may well in some cases be supposed; for the psalmist would not represent his case by what would be absurd, and to which no degree of that exercise of mind he spoke of would have any tendency.

We read of the disciples that when they saw Christ coming to them in the storm, and took him for some terrible enemy, threatening their destruction in that storm, 'they cried out for fear' (Matthew 14:26). Why then should it be thought strange that people should cry out for fear when God appears to them as a terrible enemy, and they see themselves in great danger of being swallowed up in the bottomless gulf of eternal misery? The spouse, once and again, speaks of herself as overpowered with the love of Christ, so as to weaken her body, and make her faint: 'Stay me with flagons, comfort me with apples; for I am sick of love … I charge you, O ye daughters of Jerusalem, if ye find my Beloved, that ye tell him that I am sick of love' (Song of Songs 2:5, 8). From this we may at least argue that such an effect may well be supposed to arise from such a cause in the saints in some cases, and that such an effect will sometimes be seen in the church of Christ.

It is a weak objection to say that the impressions of enthusiasts have a great effect on their bodies. That the Quakers used to tremble is no argument that Saul, afterwards called Paul, and the jailer did not tremble from real convictions of conscience. Indeed, all such objections from effects on the body, whether greater or less, seems to be exceedingly frivolous. Those who argue from them proceed in the dark – they do not know what ground they go upon, nor by what rule they judge. The root and course of things is to be looked at, and the nature of the operations and affections are to be inquired into, and examined by the rule of God's word, and not the motions of the blood and animal spirits.

Publicity

It is no argument that an operation on people's minds is not the work of the Spirit of God, that it occasions a great deal of noise about religion. For though true religion is contrary to that of the Pharisees – which was ostentatious, and delighted to set itself forth to the view of men for their applause – yet such is human nature that it is morally impossible for there to be a great concern, strong affection, and a general engagedness of mind amongst a people, without causing a notable, visible, and open commotion and alteration amongst that people. Surely, it is no argument that people's minds are not under the influence of God's Spirit, that they are very much moved; for indeed spiritual and eternal things are so great, and of such infinite concern, that there is a great absurdity in men's being only moderately moved and affected by them; and surely it is no argument that they are affected with these things in some measure as they deserve, or in some proportion to their importance. And when was there ever any such things since the world stood, as a people in general being greatly affected in any affair whatsoever, without noise or stir? The nature of man will not allow it.

Indeed, Christ says: 'The kingdom of God cometh not with observation' (Luke 17:20). That is, it will not consist in what is outward and visible; it will not be like earthly kingdoms, set up with outward pomp, in some particular place which will be the special royal city and seat of the kingdom. As Christ explains in the words which come next: 'Neither shall they say, Lo here, or lo there; for behold the kingdom of God is within you.' Not that the kingdom of God will be set up in the world on the ruin of Satan's kingdom, without a very observable great effect: a mighty change in the state of things, to the observation and astonishment of the whole world. Just such an effect as this is foretold in the prophecies of Scripture, and by Christ himself in this very passage, and indeed in his own explanation of these words: 'For as the lightning that lightneth out of one part under heaven, shineth unto another part under heaven, so shall also the Son of man be in his day' (verse 24). This is to distinguish Christ's coming to set up his kingdom from the coming of false Christs, which he tells us will be in a private manner in the deserts and in the secret chambers; whereas this event of setting up the kingdom of God would be open and public in the sight of the whole world with clear manifestation, like lightning that cannot be hidden but glares in everyone's eyes and shines from one side of heaven to the other. And we find that when Christ's kingdom came, by that remarkable outpouring of the Spirit in the apostles' days, it occasioned a great stir everywhere. What a mighty opposition was there in Jerusalem on occasion of that great effusion of the Spirit! And so in Samaria, Antioch, Ephesus, Corinth, and other places! News of the affair filled the world, and caused some people to say of the apostles that they had turned the world upside down (Acts 17:6).

The effect on people's imagination

It is no argument that an operation on people's minds is not the work of the Spirit of God, that many who are subject to it have great impressions made on their imaginations. That people have many impressions on their imaginations does not prove that they have nothing else. It is easy to account for there being much of this nature among a people, where a great many, of all kinds, have their minds engaged with intense thought and strong feelings about invisible things. Indeed, it would be strange if this did not happen. Such is our nature that we cannot think about invisible things with out a degree of imagination. I dare appeal to any man, of the greatest powers of mind, whether he is able to fix his thoughts on God or Christ, or the things of another world, without imaginary ideas attending his meditations? And the more engaged the mind is, and the more intense the contemplation and affection, still the more lively and strong the imaginary idea will ordinarily be; especially when attended with surprise. And this is the case when the mental prospect is very new, and takes strong hold of the passions, such as fear or joy; and when the state and views of the mind suddenly changes from a contrary extreme, such as from that which was extremely dreadful to that which is extremely delightful. And it is no wonder that many people do not easily distinguish between that which is imaginary and that which is intellectual and spiritual; and that they are apt to lay too much weight on the imaginary part, and are most ready to speak of that in the account they give of their experiences, especially people of less understanding and distinguishing capacity.

As God has given us such a faculty as the imagination, and so made us that we cannot think of things spiritual and invisible without some exercise of this faculty; so it appears to me that such is our state and nature that this faculty is really subservient and helpful to the other faculties of the mind, when a proper use is made of it; though often, when the imagination is too strong, and the other faculties weak, it overbears, and disturbs them in their exercise. It seems clear to me, in many instances with which I have been acquainted, that God has really made use of this faculty to truly divine purposes; especially in some that are more ignorant. God seems to condescend to their circumstances, and deal with them as babes; as of old he instructed his church, whilst in a state of ignorance and minority, by types and outward representations. I can see nothing unreasonable in such a position. Let others who have much occasion to deal with souls in spiritual concerns, judge whether experience does not confirm it.

It is no argument that a work is not of the Spirit of God, that some who are the subjects of it have been in a kind of ecstasy, in which they have had their minds transported into a train of strong and pleasing imaginations, and a kind of visions, as though they were rapt up to heaven, and there saw glorious sights. I have been acquainted with some such instances, and I see no need of bringing in the help of the devil into the account that we give of these things, nor yet of supposing them to be of the same nature as the visions of the prophets, or St Paul's rapture into paradise. Human nature, under these intense exercises and affections, is all that need be brought into the account. If it may be well accounted for, that people under a true sense of the glorious and wonderful greatness and excellence of divine things, and soul-ravishing views of the beauty and love of Christ, should have the strength of nature over-powered, as I have already shown that it may; then I think it is not at all strange that amongst great numbers that are thus affected and overborne, there should be some persons of particular constitutions that have their imaginations affected like this. The effect is no other than what bears a proportion and analogy to other effects of the strong exercise of their minds. It is no wonder, when the thoughts are so fixed, and the affections so strong – and the whole soul so engaged, ravished, and swallowed up – that all other parts of the body are so affected as to be deprived of their strength, and the whole frame ready to dissolve. Is it any wonder that, in such a case, the brain in particular (especially in some constitutions), which we know is most especially affected by intense contemplations and exercises of mind, should be so affected that its strength and spirits should be diverted for a while, and taken off from impressions made on the organs of external sense, and wholly employed in a train of pleasing delightful imaginations, corresponding with the present frame of the mind? Some people are ready to interpret such things wrongly, and to lay too much weight on them, as prophetic visions, divine revelations, and sometimes indications from heaven of what is to happen (which, in some instances I have known, have been disproved in the event). But yet it appears to me that such things are evidently sometimes from the Spirit of God, though indirectly; that is, their extraordinary frame of mind, and that strong and lively sense of divine things which is the occasion of them, is from his Spirit; and also as the mind continues in its holy frame, and retains a divine sense of the excellence of spiritual things even in its rapture; which holy frame and sense is from the Spirit of God, though the imaginations that attend it are only accidental, and therefore there is commonly something or other in them that is confused, improper, and false.

Example

It is no sign that a work is not from the Spirit of God that example is a great means of it. It is surely no argument that an effect is not from God, that means are used in producing it; for we know that it is God's manner to make use of means in carrying on his work in the world, and it is no more an argument against the divinity of an effect, that this means is made us of, than if it was by any other means. It is agreeable to Scripture that people should be influenced by one another's good example. The Scripture directs us to set good examples to that end (Matthew 5:16; 1 Peter 3:1; 1 Timothy 4:12; Titus 2:7), and also directs us to be influenced by the good examples of others, and to follow them (2 Corinthians 8: 1-7;

Hebrews 6:12; Philippians 3:17; 1 Corinthians 4:16 and 11:1; 2 Thessalonians 3:9; 1 Thessalonians 1:7). By this it appears that example is one of God's means; and certainly it is no argument that a work is not of God, that his own means are made use of to effect it.

And as it is a *scriptural* way of carrying on God's work, by example, so it is a *reasonable* way. It is no argument that men are not influenced by reason, that they are influenced by example. This way of people holding forth truth to one another has a tendency to enlighten the mind, and to convince reason. None will deny but that for people to communicate things to one another by words may rationally be supposed to tend to enlighten each other's minds; but the same thing may be communicated by actions, and much more fully and effectually. Words are of no use unless they convey our own ideas to others; but actions, in some cases, may do it much more fully. There is a language in actions; and in some cases it is much more clear and convincing than in words. It is therefore no argument against the goodness of the effect, that people are greatly affected by seeing others so; indeed, though the impression may be made only by seeing the tokens of great and extraordinary affection in others in their behaviour, taking for granted what they are affected with, without hearing them say one word. There may be language sufficient in such a case in their behaviour alone, to convey their minds to others, and to communicate their sense of things more than can possibly be done by words alone. If a person should see another under extreme bodily torment, he might receive much clearer ideas, and more convincing evidence of what he suffered by his actions in his misery, than he could do only by the words of an unaffected, indifferent relater. In like manner he might receive a greater idea of anything that is excellent and very delightful, from the behaviour of one that is in actual enjoyment, than by the dull narration of one who is inexperienced and insensible himself. I desire that this matter may be examined by the strictest reason. Is it not manifest that effects produced in people's minds are rational, since not only weak and ignorant people are much influenced by example, but also those who make the greatest boast of strength of reason, are more influenced by reason held forth in this way than almost any other way? Indeed, the religious affections of many when raised by this means (such as by hearing the word preached, or any other means) may prove flashy, and soon vanish, as Christ represents the stony-ground hearers; but the affections of some thus moved by example are abiding, and prove to result in salvation.

There never yet was a time of remarkable pouring out of the Spirit, and great revival of religion, but that example had a main hand. So it was at the reformation, and in the apostles' days in Jerusalem and Samaria and Ephesus, and other parts of the world, as will be most manifest to anyone who attends to the accounts we have in the Acts of the Apostles. As in those days one person was moved by another, so one city or town was influenced by the example of another: 'So that ye were ensamples to all that believe in Macedonia and Achaia, for from you sounded out the word of the Lord, not only in Macedonia and Achaia, but also in every place your faith to God-ward is spread abroad' (1 Thessalonians 1:7-8).

It is no valid objection against example being so much used, that the Scripture speaks of the words as the principal means of carrying on God's work; for the word of God is the principal means, nevertheless, by which other means operate and are made effectual. Even the sacraments have no effect except by the word; and so it is that example becomes effectual; for all that is visible to the eye is unintelligible and vain without the word of God to instruct and guide the mind. It is the word of God that is indeed held forth and applied by example, as the word of the Lord sounded forth to other towns in Macedonia and Achaia by the example of those who believed in Thessalonica.

That example should be a great means of propagating the church of God seems to be indicated in Scripture in several ways: it is indicated by Ruth's following Naomi out of the land of Moab, into the land of Israel, when she resolved that she would not leave her, but would go wherever she went, and would lodge where she lodged; and that Naomi's people would be her people, and Naomi's

God, her God. Ruth, who was the ancestral mother of David, and of Christ, was undoubtedly a great type of the church; and for this reason her story is inserted in the canon of Scripture. In her leaving the land of Moab and its gods to come and put her trust under the shadow of the wings of the God of Israel, we have a type of the conversion not only of the Gentile church but of every sinner, that is naturally an alien and stranger, but in his conversion forgets his own people, and father's house, and becomes a fellow-citizen with the saints and a true Israelite.

The same seems to be indicated in the effect which the example of the lovesick spouse has on the daughters of Jerusalem, i.e., visible Christians, who are first awakened by seeing the spouse in such extraordinary circumstances, and then converted (see Song of Songs 5:8-9 and 6:1). And this is undoubtedly one way that 'the Spirit and the bride say, come' (Revelation 22:17) – i.e., the Spirit in the bride. It is foretold that the work of God will be very much carried on by this means in the last great outpouring of the Spirit that will introduce the glorious day of the church, so often spoke of in Scripture: 'And the inhabitants of one city shall go to another, saying, Let us go speedily to pray before the Lord, and to seek the Lord of hosts: I will go also. Yea, many people, and strong nations, shall come to seek the Lord of hosts in Jerusalem, and to pray before the Lord. Thus saith the Lord of hosts, In those days it shall come to pass, that ten men shall take hold of the skirt of him that is a Jew, saying, We will go with you for we have heard that God is with you' (Zechariah 8:21-23).

Human faults

It is no sign that a work is not from the Spirit of God, that many people who seem to be the subjects of it are guilty of great imprudences and irregularities in the conduct. We are to consider that the end for which God pours out his Spirit is to make men holy, and not to make them politic. It is no wonder that, in a mixed multitude of all sorts – wise and unwise, young and old, of weak and strong natural abilities, under strong impressions of mind – there are many who behave imprudently. There are but few who know how to conduct themselves under strong feelings of any kind, whether of a temporal or spiritual nature; to do so requires a great deal of discretion, strength, and steadiness of mind. A thousand imprudences will not prove a work to be not of the Spirit of God; indeed, if there are not only imprudences but many things prevailing that are irregular, and really contrary to the rule of God's holy word. That it should be like this may be accounted for by the exceeding weakness of human nature, together with the remaining darkness and corruption of those that are the subjects of the saving influence of God's Spirit, and have a real zeal for God.

We have a remarkable instance, in the New Testament, of a people that partook largely of that great effusion of the Spirit in the apostles' days, among whom there nevertheless abounded imprudence and great irregularities; namely, the church at Corinth. There is scarcely any church more celebrated in the New Testament for being blessed with large measures of the Spirit of God, both in his ordinary influences, in convincing and converting sinners, and also in his extraordinary and miraculous gifts; yet what manifold imprudences, great and sinful irregularities, and strange confusion did they run into, at the Lord's supper, and in the exercise of church discipline! To which may be added their indecent manner of attending other parts of public worship, their jarring and contention about their teachers, and even the exercise of their extraordinary gifts of prophecy, speaking with tongues, and the like, in which they spoke and acted by the immediate inspiration of the Spirit of God.

And if we see great imprudences, and even sinful irregularities, in some who are great instruments to carry on the work, it will not prove it not to be the work of God. The apostle Peter himself, who was a great, eminently holy, and inspired apostle – and one of the chief instruments of setting up the Christian church in the world – when he was actually engaged in this work was guilty of a great and sinful error in his conduct; of which the apostle Paul speaks in

Galatians 2:11-13: 'But when Peter was come to Antioch, I withstood him to the face, because he was to be blamed; for before that certain men came from James, he did eat with the Gentiles, but when they were come, he withdrew, and separated himself, fearing them that were of the circumcision; and the other Jews dissembled likewise with him; insomuch, that Barnabas also was carried away with their dissimulation.' If a great pillar of the Christian church — one of the chief of those who are the very foundations on which, next to Christ, the whole church is said to be built — was guilty of such an irregularity, is it any wonder if other lesser instruments, who have not that extraordinary conduct of the divine Spirit he had, should be guilty of many irregularities?

And in particular, it is no evidence that a work is not of God, if many who are either the subjects or the instruments of it are guilty of too great forwardness to censure others as unconverted. For this may be through mistakes they have embraced concerning the marks by which they are to judge of the hypocrisy and carnality of others; or from not duly apprehending the latitude the Spirit of God uses in the methods of his operations; or, from not making due allowance for that infirmity and corruption that may be left in the hearts of the saints; as well as through lack of a due sense of their own blindness and weakness, and remaining corruption, by which spiritual pride may have a secret vent this way, under some disguise, and not be discovered. If we admit that truly pious men may have a great deal of remaining blindness and corruption, and may be liable to mistakes about the marks of hypocrisy, as undoubtedly all will agree, then it is not unaccountable that they should sometimes run into such errors as these. It is easy, and upon some accounts more easy to be accounted for, why the remaining corruption of good men should sometimes have an unobserved vent like this, than in most other ways; and without doubt (however lamentable) many holy men have erred in this way.

Lukewarmness in religion is abominable, and zeal an excellent grace; yet above all other Christian virtues, this needs to be strictly watched and searched; for it is that with which corruption, and particularly pride and human passion, is exceedingly apt to mix unobserved. And it is observable that there never was a time of great reformation, to cause a revival of zeal in the church of God, that has not been attended in some notable instances with irregularity, and undue severity in one way or another. Thus in the apostles' days, a great deal of zeal was spent about unclean foods, with heat of spirit in Christians against one another, both parties condemning and censuring one another as not true Christians; when the apostle had charity for both, as influenced by a spirit of real piety: 'he that eats', he says, 'to the Lord he eats, and giveth God thanks; and he that eateth not, to the Lord he eateth not, and giveth God thanks.' So in the church of Corinth, they had got into a way of extolling some ministers, and censuring others, and were puffed up against one another; but yet these things were no sign that the work then so wonderfully carried on was not the work of God. And after this, when religion was still greatly flourishing in the world, and a spirit of eminent holiness and zeal prevailed in the Christian church, the zeal of Christians ran out into a very improper and undue severity, in the exercise of church discipline towards delinquets. In some cases they would by no means admit them into their charity and communion though they appeared never so humble and penitent. And in the days of Constantine the Great, the zeal of Christians against heathenism overflowed into a degree of persecution. Similarly in that glorious revival of religion, at the reformation, zeal in many instances appeared in a very improper severity, and even a degree of persecution; indeed, in some of the most eminent reformers, such as the great Calvin in particular. And many in those days of the flourishing of vital religion were guilty of severely censuring others who differed from them in opinion in some points of divinity.

Errors and delusions

Nor are many errors of judgement, and some delusions of Satan intermixed with the work, any argument that the work in-general is not of the Spirit of God. However great a spiritual influence may be, it is not to be expected that the Spirit of God should be given now in the same manner as to the apostles, infallibly to guide them in points of Christian doctrine, so that what they taught might be relied on as a rule to the Christian church. And if many delusions of Satan appear at the same time that a great religious concern prevails, it is not an argument that the work in general is not the work of God, any more than it was an argument that in Egypt that there were no true miracles wrought there by the hand of God, because Jannes and Jambres wrought false miracles at the same time by the hand of the devil. Indeed, the same persons may be the subjects of much of the influences of the Spirit of God, and yet in some things be led away by the delusions of Satan, and this be no more of paradox than many other things that are true of real saints, in the present state, where grace dwells with so much corruption, and the new man and the old man subsist together in the same person; and the kingdom of God and the kingdom of the devil remain for a while together in the same heart. Many godly persons have undoubtedly in this and other ages exposed themselves to woeful delusions by an aptness to lay too much weight on impulses and impressions, as if they were immediate revelations from God, to signify something future, or to direct them where to go, and what to do.

Counterfeits

If some who were thought to be wrought upon fall away into gross errors, or scandalous practices, it is no argument that the work in general is not the work of the Spirit of God. That there are some counterfeits is no argument that nothing is true: such things are always expected in a time of reformation. If we look into church history, we shall find no instance of any great revival of religion but what has been attended with many such things. Instances of this nature in the apostles' days were innumerable; some fell away into gross heresies, others into vile practices, though they seemed to be the subjects of a work of the Spirit – and were accepted for a while amongst those that were truly so as their brethren and companions – and were not suspected till they went out from them. And some of these were teachers and officers – and eminent persons in the Christian church – whom God had endowed with miraculous gifts of the Holy Spirit; as appears from the beginning of Hebrews 6.

An instance of these was Judas, who was one of the twelve apostles, and had long been constantly united to, and intimately conversant with, a company of disciples of true experience, without being discovered or suspected, till he revealed himself by his scandalous practice. He had been treated by Jesus himself, in all external things, as if he had truly been a disciple, even investing him with the character of apostle, sending him out to preach the gospel, and enduing him with miraculous gifts of the Spirit. For though Christ knew him, yet he did not then clothe himself with the character of omniscient Judge and searcher of hearts, but acted the part of a minister of the visible church (for he was his Father's minister); and therefore did not reject him till he had revealed himself by his scandalous practice; thereby giving an example to guides and rulers of the visible church, not to take it upon themselves to act the part of searcher of hearts, but to be influenced in their administrations by what is visible and open.

There were some instances then of such apostates, who were esteemed eminently full of the grace of God's Spirit. An instance of this nature probably was Nicolas, one of the seven deacons, who was looked upon by the Christians in Jerusalem, in the time of that extraordinary outpouring of the Spirit, as a man full of the Holy Spirit, and was chosen out of the multitude of Christians for that office for that reason (Acts 6:3, 5); yet he afterwards fell away and became the head of a sect of vile heretics, of gross practices, called from his name the sect of the Nicolaitans (Revelation 2:6; 15).

So in the time of the reformation, how great was the number of those who for a while seemed to join with the reformers, yet fell away into the grossest and most absurd errors, and abominable practices. And it is particularly observable that in times of great pouring out of the Spirit to revive religion in the world, a number of those who for a while seemed to partake in it, have fallen off into whimsical and extravagant errors, and gross enthusiasm, boasting of high degrees of spirituality and perfection, censuring and condemning others as carnal. Thus it was with the Gnostics in the apostles' times; and thus it was with several sects at the reformation, as Anthony Burgess observes:

> The first worthy reformers, and glorious instruments of God, found a bitter conflict herein, so that they were exercised not only with formalists, and traditionary papists on the one side, but men that pretended themselves to be more enlightened than the reformers were, on the other side: hence they called those that did adhere to the Scripture, and would try revelations by it, Literists and Vowelists, as men acquainted with the words and vowels of Scripture, having nothing of the Spirit of God: and wheresoever in any town, the true doctrine of the gospel brake forth to the displacing of popery, presently such opinions arose, like tares that came up among the good wheat; whereby great divisions were raised, and the reformation made abominable and odious to the world; as if that had been the sun to give heat and warmth to those worms and serpents to crawl out of the ground. Hence they inveighed against Luther, and said he had only promulgated a carnal gospel. (*Spiritual Refinings* I.23, p.132)

Some of the leaders of those wild enthusiasts had been for a while highly esteemed by the first reformers, and peculiarly dear to them.

Thus also in England, at the time when vital religion much prevailed in the days of King Charles I, the interregnum, and Oliver Cromwell, such things as these abounded. And so in New England in her purest days, when vital piety flourished, such kind of things as these broke out. Therefore the devil's sowing such tares is no proof that a true work of the Spirit of God is not gloriously carried on.

Hell-fire preaching

It is no argument that a work is not from the Spirit of God, that it seems to be promoted by ministers insisting very much on the terrors of God's holy law, and that with a great deal of pathos and earnestness. If there really is a hell of such dreadful and never-ending torments as is generally supposed, of which multitudes are in great danger – and into which the greater part of men in Christian countries do actually from generation to generation fall, for lack of a sense of its terribleness, and so for lack of taking due care to avoid it – then why is it not proper for those who have the care of souls to take great pains to make men aware of it? Why should they not be told as much of the truth as can be? If I am in danger of going to hell, I should be glad to know as much as I possibly can of the dreadfulness of it. If I am very prone to neglect due care to avoid it, the person who does me the best kindness is he who does most to represent to me the truth of the case, setting forth my misery and danger in the liveliest manner.

I ask everyone whether this is not the very course they would take in case of exposure to any great temporal calamity. If any of you who are heads of families saw your children in a house all on fire, and in imminent danger of soon being consumed in the flames, yet seemed to be very unaware of its danger, and neglected to escape after you had often called them – would you go on to speak only in a cold and indifferent manner? Would you not cry aloud, and call earnestly, and tell them the danger they were in, and their folly in delaying, in the most lively manner of which you were capable? Would not nature itself teach this, and oblige you to do so? If you continued to speak only in a cold manner, as you usually do in ordinary conversation about indifferent matters, would not those about you begin to think that you were bereft of reason yourself? This is not the way of mankind in temporal affairs of great moment, that require earnest heed and great haste, and about which they are greatly concerned. They do not usually speak to others of their danger, and warn them just a little, or in a cold and indifferent manner. Nature teaches men otherwise. If we who have the care of souls knew what hell was, had seen the state of the damned or by any other means had become

41

aware how dreadful their case was – and at the same time knew that most people went there, and saw our hearers not aware of their danger – it would be morally impossible for us to avoid most earnestly setting before them the dreadfulness of that misery, and their great exposedness to it, and even to cry aloud to them.

When ministers preach about hell, and warn sinners to avoid it, in a cold manner – though they may say in words that it is infinitely terrible – they contradict themselves. For actions, as I observed before, have a language as well as words. If a preacher's words represent the sinner's state as infinitely dreadful, while his behaviour and manner of speaking contradict it – showing that the preacher does not think so – he defeats his own purpose; for the language of his actions in such a case is much more effectual than the bare meaning of his words. Not that I think that the law only should be preached: ministers may preach other things too little. The gospel is to be preached as well as the law, and the law is to be preached only to make way for the gospel, and in order that it may be preached more effectually. The main work of ministers is to preach the gospel: 'Christ is the end of the law for righteousness'. So a minister would miss it very much if he should insist so much on the terrors of the law as to forget his Lord, and neglect to preach the gospel; but the law is still very much to be insisted on, and the preaching of the gospel will probably be in vain without it.

And certainly such earnestness and affection in speaking is beautiful, as becomes the nature and importance of the subject. Not but that there may be such a thing as an indecent boisterousness in a preacher, something besides which the matter and manner do not well agree together. Some people talk of it as an unreasonable thing to frighten people to heaven; but I think it is a reasonable thing to endeavour to frighten people away from hell. They stand upon its brink, and are just ready to fall into it, and are unaware of their danger. Is it not a reasonable thing to frighten a person out of a house on fire? The word 'fright' is commonly used for sudden, causeless fear, or groundless surprise; but surely a fear for which there is good reason is not to be criticized by any such name.

The distinguishing marks of
a work of the Spirit of God:
Part 2

Scripture evidences

Having given some examples of things that are not evidence that a work wrought among a people is not a work of the Spirit of God, I now proceed to show positively what are the sure, distinguishing scripture evidences and marks of a work of the Spirit of God, by which we may proceed in judging any operation we find in ourselves, or see among a people, without danger of being misled. And in this, as I said before, I shall confine myself to those marks which are given us by the apostle in 1 John 4, where this matter is dealt with particularly, and more plainly and fully than anywhere else in the Bible. And in speaking about these marks, I shall take them in the order in which I find them in the chapter.

Confirming the gospel of Jesus as Son of God

When the operation is such as to raise their esteem of that Jesus who was born of the Virgin, and was crucified outside the gates of Jerusalem; and seems more to confirm and establish their minds in the truth of what the gospel declares to us of his being the Son of God, and the Saviour of men, this is a sure sign that it is from the Spirit of God. The apostle gives us this sign in verses 2 and 3:

'Hereby know ye the Spirit of God; and every spirit that confesseth that Jesus Christ is come in the flesh is of God; and every spirit that confesseth not that Jesus Christ is come in the flesh is not of God.' This implies a confessing not only that there was such a person who appeared in Palestine and did and suffered those things that are recorded of him, but that he was the Christ, i.e. the Son of God, anointed to be Lord and Saviour, as the name Jesus Christ implies. That thus much is implied in the apostle's meaning is confirmed by verse 15, where the apostle is still on the same subject of signs of the true Spirit: 'Whosoever shall confess that Jesus is the Son of God, God dwelleth in him, and he in God.' And it is to be observed that the word *confess*, as it is often used in the New Testament, signifies more than merely *allowing*: it implies an establishing and confirming of a thing by testimony, and declaring it with manifestation of esteem and affection. 'Whosoever therefore shall *confess* me before men, him will I *confess* also before my Father which is in heaven' (Matthew 10:32). 'I will *confess* to thee among the Gentiles, and sing unto thy name' (Romans 15:9). 'That every tongue shall *confess* that Jesus Christ is Lord, to the glory of God the Father' (Philippians 2:11). And that this is the force of the expression as the apostle John uses it in this passage is confirmed in the next chapter, verse 1: 'Whosoever believeth that Jesus is the Christ, is born of God, and every one that loveth him that begat, loveth him also that is begotten of him.' And by that parallel passage of the apostle Paul, where we have the same rule given to distinguish the true Spirit from all counterfeits: 'Wherefore I give you to understand that no man speaking by the Spirit of God, calleth Jesus accursed [or will show an ill or mean esteem of him]; and that no man can say that Jesus is the Lord, but by the Holy Ghost' (1 Corinthians 21:3).

So if the spirit that is at work among a people is plainly observed to work so as to convince them of Christ, and lead them to him – to confirm their minds in the belief of the history of Christ as he appeared in the flesh – and that he is the Son of God, and was sent by God to save sinners; that he is the only Saviour, and that they stand in great need of him; and if he seems to beget in them higher and more honourable thoughts of him than they used to have and to incline their affections more to him; it is a sure sign that it is the true and right Spirit; however incapable we may be of determining whether that conviction and affection is in that manner, or to that degree, as to be saving or not.

But the words of the apostle are remarkable; the person to whom the Spirit gives testimony, and for whom he raises their esteem, must be that Jesus who appeared in the flesh, and not another Christ in his stead; nor any mystical, fantastical Christ, such as the light within. The spirit of Quakers extols this, while it diminishes their esteem of and dependence upon an outward Christ – or Jesus as he came in the flesh – and leads them off from him; but the spirit that gives testimony for that Jesus, and leads to him, can be no other than the Spirit of God. The devil has the most bitter and implacable enmity against that person, especially in his character of the Saviour of men; he mortally hates the story and doctrine of his redemption; he never would go about to beget in men and more honourable thoughts of him, and lay greater weight on his instructions and commands. The Spirit that inclines men's hearts to the seed of the woman is not the spirit of the serpent that has such a irreconcilable enmity against him. He that heightens men's esteem of the glorious Michael, that prince of the angels, is not the spirit of the dragon that is at war with him.

Working against sin

When the spirit that is at work operates against the interests of Satan's kingdom, which lies in encouraging and establishing sin, and cherishing men's worldly lusts, this is a sure sign that it is a true, and not a false spirit. This sign we have given us in verses 4 and 5: 'Ye are of God, little children, and have overcome them; because greater is he that is in you, than he that is in the world. They are of the world, therefore speak they of the world, and the world heareth them.' Here is a plain antithesis: it is evident that the apostle is still comparing those that are influenced by the two opposite kinds of spirits, the true and the false, and showing the difference; the one is of God, and overcomes the spirit of the world; the other is of the world, and speaks and savours the things of the world. The spirit of the devil is here called 'he that is in the world'. Christ says, 'My kingdom is not of this world'. But it is otherwise with Satan's kingdom; he is 'the god of this world'.

What the apostle means by the *world*, or 'the things that are of the world', we learn by his own words in 1 John 2:15-16: 'Love not the world, neither the things that are in the world: if any man love the world, the love of the Father is not in him: for all that is in the world, the lust of the flesh, and the lust of the eyes, and the pride of life, is not of the Father, but is of the world.' So by the world the apostle evidently means everything that appertains to the interest of sin, and comprehends all the corruptions and lusts of men, and all those acts and objects by which they are gratified.

So we may safely determine from what the apostle says that the spirit that is at work amongst a people, after such a manner as to lessen their esteem of the pleasures, profits, and honours of the world, and to take off their hearts from an eager pursuit after these things; and to engage them in a deep concern about a future state and eternal happiness which the gospel reveals – and puts them upon earnestly seeking the kingdom of God and his righteousness; and the spirit that convinces them of the dreadfulness of sin, the guilt it brings, and the misery to which it exposes – this must be the Spirit of God.

It is not to be supposed that Satan would convince men of sin, and awaken the conscience; it can no way serve his end to make that candle of the Lord shine the brighter, and to open the mouth of that vicegerent of God in the soul. It is for his interest, whatever he does, to lull conscience asleep, and keep it quiet. To have that, with its eyes and mouth open in the soul, will tend to clog and hinder all his desires of darkness, and evermore to disturb his affairs, to cross his interest, and disquiet him, so that he can achieve nothing he wants without being molested. Would the devil, when he is trying to establish men in sin, take such a course, in the first place, to enlighten and awaken the conscience to see the dreadfulness of sin, and make them exceedingly afraid of it, and aware of their misery by reason of their past sins, and their great need of deliverance from their guilt? Would he make them more careful, inquisitive, and watchful to discern what is sinful, and to avoid future sins, and so be more afraid of the devil's temptations, and more careful to guard against them? What do those men do with their reason, who suppose that the Spirit that operates thus is the spirit of the devil?

Possibly some may say that the devil may even awaken men's consciences to deceive them, and make them think they have been the subject of a saving work of the Spirit of God, while they are indeed still in the gall of bitterness. But to this it may be replied that the man who has an awakened conscience is the least likely to be deceived by anyone in the world; it is the drowsy, unaware, stupid conscience that is most easily blinded. The more aware conscience is in a diseased soul, the less easily is it quieted without a real healing. The more aware conscience is made of the dreadfulness of sin, and of the greatness of a man's own guilt, the less likely he is to rest in his own righteousness, or to be pacified with nothing but shadows. A man that has been thoroughly terrified with a sense of his own danger and misery is not easily flattered and made to believe himself safe, without any good grounds. To awaken conscience, and convince it of the evil of sin, cannot tend to establish it, but certainly tends to make way for sin and Satan's being cut out. Therefore this is a good argument that the Spirit that operates in this way cannot be but the spirit of the devil – unless we suppose that Christ did not know how to argue, when he told the Pharisees (who supposed that the Spirit by which he worked was the spirit of the devil) that Satan would not cast out Satan (Matthew 12:25-26). And therefore, if we see people made aware of the dreadful nature of sin, and of the displeasure of God against it; of their own miserable condition as they are in themselves, by reason of sin, and earnestly concerned for their eternal salvation – and aware of their need of God's pity and help, and committed to seek it in the use of the means that God has appointed – we may certainly conclude that it is from the Spirit of God, whatever effects this concern has on their bodies – even if it causes them to cry out aloud, or to shriek, or to faint; or if it throws them into convulsions, or whatever other way the blood and spirits are moved.

The influence of the Spirit of God is yet more abundantly manifest if people have their hearts drawn away from the world, and weaned from the objects of their worldly lusts, and away from worldly pursuits, by the feelings they have for those spiritual enjoyments of another world, that are promised in the gospel.

Enhancing regard for the Scriptures

The spirit that operates in such a manner as to cause in men a greater regard for the Holy Scriptures, and establishes them more in their truth and divinity, is certainly the Spirit of God. The apostle gives us this rule in verse 6: 'We are of God; he that knoweth God heareth us; he that is not of God heareth not us: hereby know we the spirit of truth, and the spirit of error.' *We are of God*; that is, 'We the apostles are sent forth by God, and appointed by him to teach the world, and to deliver those doctrines and instructions which are to be their rule; *he that knoweth God, heareth us...*'

The apostle's argument here equally reaches all that in the same sense are *of God*; that is, all those that God has appointed and inspired to deliver to his church its rule of faith and practice; all the prophets and apostles, whose doctrine God has made the foundation on which he has built his church, as in Ephesians 2:20 – in a word, all the penmen of the Holy Scriptures. The devil would never attempt to beget in people a regard for that divine word which God has given to be the great and standing rule for the direction of his church in all religious matters, and all concerns of their souls, in all ages. A spirit of delusion will not incline people to seek direction at the mouth of God. 'To the law and to the testimony' is never the cry of those evil spirits that have no light in them; for it is God's own direction to discover their delusions. 'And when they

48

shall say unto you, Seek unto them that have familiar spirits, and unto wizards that peep and that mutter: should not a people seek unto their God? for the living to the dead? To the law and to the testimony; if they speak not according to this word, it is because there is no light in them' (Isaiah 8:19-20). The devil does not say the same as Abraham did – 'They have Moses and the prophets, let them hear them' – nor the same as the voice from heaven did concerning Christ – 'Hear ye him'. Would the spirit of error, in order to deceive people, beget in them a high opinion of the infallible rule, and incline them to think a lot about it, and be very conversant with it? Would the prince of darkness, in order to promote his kingdom of darkness, lead men to the sun? The devil has always shown a mortal spite and hatred towards that holy book the Bible; he has done all in his power to extinguish that light, and to lead people away from it. He knows it to be that light by which his kingdom of darkness is to be overthrown. He has had for many ages experience of its power to defeat his purposes, and baffle his designs; it is his constant plague. It is the main weapon which Michael uses in his war with him; it is the sword of the Spirit, that pierces him and conquers him. It is that great and strong word with which God punishes Leviathan, that crooked serpent. It is that sharp sword that we read of in Revelation 19:15, that proceeds out of the mouth of him that sat on the horse, with which he smites his enemies. Every text is a dart to torment the old serpent. He has felt the stinging dart thousands of times; therefore he is against the Bible, and hates every word in it; and we may be sure he will never attempt to raise people's esteem of it or feeling for it. And accordingly we see it common in enthusiasts, that they depreciate this written rule, and set up the light within or some other rule above it.

Leading people to the truth

Another rule to judge spirits by may be drawn from the names given to the opposite spirits, in the last words of verse 6: 'the spirit of truth and the spirit of error'. These words exhibit the two opposite characters of the Spirit of God, and other spirits that counterfeit his operations. And therefore, if by observing the manner of the operation of a spirit that is at work among a people, we see that it operates as a spirit of truth, leading people to truth, convincing them of those things that are true, we may safely determine that it is a right and true spirit. For instance, if we observe that the spirit at work makes people more aware than they used to be that there is a God, and that he is a great and a sin-hating God; that life is short, and very uncertain; and that there is another world; that they have immortal souls, and must give account of themselves to God, that they are exceedingly sinful by nature and practice; that they are helpless in themselves; and confirms them in other things that agree with some sound doctrine; the spirit that works in such a way operates as a spirit of truth; he represents things as they truly are. He brings people to the light; for whatever makes truth manifest is light; as the apostle Paul observes: 'But all things that are reproved [or discovered, as it is in the margin] are made manifest by the light; for whatsoever doth make manifest is light' (Ephesians 5:13). And therefore we may conclude that it is not the spirit of darkness that thus reveals the truth and makes it clear. Christ tells us that Satan is a liar, and the father of lies; and his kingdom is a kingdom of darkness. It is upheld and promoted only by darkness and error. Satan has all his power and dominion by darkness. Hence we read of the power of darkness (Luke 22:53 and Colossians 1:13). And devils are called 'the rulers of the darkness of this world'. Whatever spirit removes our darkness, and brings us to the light, undeceives us, and, by convincing us of the truth, does us a kindness. If I am brought to a sight of truth, and made aware of things as they really are, my duty is immediately to thank God for it, without stopping first to inquire by what means I have such a benefit.

Operating as a spirit of love

If the spirit that is at work among a people operates as a spirit of love to God and man, it is a sure sign that it is the Spirit of God.

The apostle insists on this sign from verse 6 to the end of the chapter: 'Beloved, let us love one another; for love is of God, and every one that loveth is born of God, and knoweth God: he that loveth not, knoweth not God; for God is love…' Here it is evident that the apostle is still comparing those low sorts of people that are influenced by the opposite kinds of spirits; and he mentioned love as a mark by which we may know who has the true spirit. This is especially evident from verses 12 and 13: 'If we love one another, God dwelleth in us, and his love is perfected in us: hereby know we that we dwell in him, and he in us, because he hath given us of his Spirit.' In these verses love is spoken of as if it were that in which the very nature of the Holy Spirit consisted; or as if *divine love* dwelling in us, and the *Spirit of God* dwelling in us, were the same thing. It is the same in the last two verses of the previous chapter, and verse 16 of this chapter. Therefore this last mark which the apostle gives of the true Spirit he seems to speak of as the most eminent; and so insists much more largely upon it than upon all the rest; and speaks expressly of both love to God and love to men – of *love to men* in verses 7, 11, and 12; and of *love to God* in verses 17, 18, and 19; and of both together in the last two verses; and of love to men as arising from love to God, in these last two verses.

Therefore, when the spirit that is at work amongst the people tends this way, and brings many of them to high and exalting thoughts of the Divine Being, and his glorious perfections; and works in them an admiring, delightful sense of the excellence of Jesus Christ; representing him as the chief among ten thousand, and altogether lovely; and makes him precious to the soul, winning and drawing the heart with those motives and incitements to love, of which the apostle speaks in that passage of Scripture we are upon, namely the wonderful, free love of God in giving his only-begotten Son to die for us, and the wonderful love of Christ to us, who had no love to him, but were his enemies – this must be the Spirit of God. 'In this was manifested the love of God towards us, because God sent his only-begotten Son into the world, that we might live through him. Herein is love; not that we loved God, but

51

that he loved us, and sent his Son to be the propitiation for our sins' (verses 9-10). 'And we have known, and believed, the love that God hath to us' (verse 16). 'We love him because he first loved us' (verse 19). The spirit that excites people to love on these motives, and makes the attributes of God as revealed in the gospel, and manifested in Christ, delightful objects of contemplation; and makes the soul long after God and Christ – after their presence and communion, acquaintance with them, and conformity to them – and to live so as to please and honour them – the spirit that quells contentions among men, and gives a spirit of peace and good will, excites to acts of outward kindness, and earnest desires of the salvation of souls – and causes a delight in those that appear as the children of God, and followers of Christ; I say, when a spirit operates in this way among a people, there is the highest kind of evidence of the influence of a true and divine spirit.

Indeed there is a counterfeit love, that often appears among those who are led by a spirit of delusion. There is commonly in the wildest enthusiasts a kind of union and affection arising from self-love, occasioned by their agreeing in those things in which they greatly differ from all others, and from which they are objects of the ridicule of all the rest of mankind. This naturally will cause them so much the more to prize those peculiarities that make them the objects of others' contempt. Thus the ancient Gnostics, and the wild fanatics that appeared at the beginning of the reformation, boasted of their great love to one another; one sect of them, in particular, calling themselves the *family of love.* But this is quite another thing than that Christian love I have just described: it is only the working of a natural self-love, and no true benevolence, any more than the union and friendship which may be among a company of pirates that are at war with all the rest of the world. There is enough said in this passage about the nature of a truly Christian love, thoroughly to distinguish it from all such counterfeits. It is love that arises from apprehension of the wonderful riches of the free grace and sovereignty of God's love to us, in Christ Jesus; being attended with a sense of our own utter unworthiness, as in ourselves the enemies and haters of God and Christ, and with a renunciation of all our own excellence and righteousness. See verses 9-11 and 19. The surest character of true divine supernatural love – distinguishing it from counterfeits that arise from a natural self-love – is that the Christian virtue of *humility* shines in it; that which above all other renounces, abases, and annihilates what we term *self*. Christian love, or true charity, is a humble love. 'Charity vaunteth not itself, is not puffed up, doth not behave itself unseemly, seeketh not her own, is not easily provoked' (1 Corinthians 13:4-5). When therefore we see love in people attended with a sense of their own littleness, vileness, weakness, and utter unsufficiency; and so with self-diffidence, self-emptiness, self-renunciation, and poverty of spirit; these are the manifest tokens of the Spirit of God. He that thus dwells in love, dwells in God, and God in him. What the apostle speaks of as a great evidence of the true Spirit, is God's love or Christ's love: 'his love is perfected in us' (verse 12). What kind of love that is, we may see best in what appeared in Christ's example. The love that appeared in that Lamb of God was not only a love to friends, but to enemies, and a love attended with a meek and humble spirit. 'Learn of me,' he says, 'for I am meek and lowly in heart.'

Love and humility are two of the most contrary things in the world to the spirit of the devil, for the character of that evil spirit, above all things, consists in pride and malice.

Thus I have spoken particularly about the various marks the apostle gives us of a work of the true Spirit. There are some of these things which the devil *would not* do if he could: thus he would not awaken the conscience, and make people aware of their miserable state because of sin, and aware of their great need of a Saviour; and he would not confirm people in the belief that Jesus is the Son of God, and the Saviour of sinners, or raise people's value and esteem of him: he would not beget in men's minds an opinion of the necessity, usefulness, and truth of the Holy Scriptures, or incline them to make much use of them; nor would he show people the truth in things that concern their souls' interest; to undeceive them and lead them out of darkness into light, and give them a view of things as they really are. And there are other things that the devil *neither can nor will* do; he will not give people a spirit of divine love, or Christian humility and poverty of spirit; nor *could* he if he wanted to. He cannot give those things he does not himself have: these things are as contrary as possible to his nature. And therefore when there is an extraordinary influence or operation appearing on the minds of a people, if these things are found in it, we are safe in determining that it is the work of God, whatever other circumstances it may be attended with, whatever instruments are used, whatever methods are taken to promote it; whatever means a sovereign God, whose judgements are a great deep, employs to carry it on; and whatever motion there may be of the animal spirits, whatever effects may be wrought on men's bodies.

These marks that the apostles have given us are sufficient to stand alone, and support themselves. They plainly show the finger of God, and are sufficient to outweigh a thousand such little objections as many make from oddities, irregularities, errors in conduct, and the delusions and scandals of some who claim to believe.

But some people may raise as an objection to the sufficiency of the marks what the apostle Paul says in 2 Corinthians 11:13-14: 'For such are false apostles, deceitful workers, transforming themselves into the apostles of Christ; and no marvel, for Satan himself is transformed into an angel of light.'

To this, I answer that this can be no objection against the sufficiency of these marks to distinguish the true from the false spirit, in those false apostles and prophets in whom the devil was transformed into an angel of light, because it is principally with a view to them that the apostle gives these marks; as appears by the words of the text, 'Believe not every spirit, but try the spirits, whether they are of God'. This is the reason he gives – because many false prophets are gone out into the world: 'There are many gone out into the world who are the ministers of the devil, who transform themselves into the prophets of God, in whom the spirit of the devil is transformed into an angel of light; therefore try the spirits by these rules that I shall give you, that you may be able to distinguish the true spirit from the false, under such a crafty disguise. Those *false prophets* the apostle John speaks of are doubtless the same sort of men as those *false apostles* and deceitful workers that the apostle Paul speaks of, in whom the devil was transformed into an angel of light; and therefore we may be sure that these marks are especially adapted to distinguish between the true Spirit, and the devil transformed into an angel of light, because they are given especially for that end; that is the apostle's declared purpose and design, to give marks by which the true Spirit may be distinguished from that sort of counterfeits.

And if we look over what is said about these false prophets, and false apostles (as there is much said about them in the New Testament), and take notice in what manner the devil was transformed into an angel of light in them, we shall not find anything that in the least injures the sufficiency of these marks to distinguish the true Spirit from such counterfeits. The devil transformed himself into an angel of light, as there was in them a show and great boast of extraordinary knowledge in divine things (Colossians 2:8; 1 Timothy 1:6-7 and 6:3-5; 2 Timothy 2:14-18; Titus 1:10, 16). Hence their followers called themselves Gnostics, from their great pretended knowledge: and the devil in them mimicked the miraculous gifts of the Holy Spirit, in visions, prophecies, miracles, etc. Hence they are called false apostles, and false prophets (Matthew 24:24). Again, there was a false show of, and lying pretensions to, great holiness and devotion in words (Romans 16:17-18; Ephesians 4:14). Hence they are called deceitful workers, and wells and clouds without water (2 Corinthians 11:13; 2 Peter 2:17; Jude 12). There was also in them a show of extraordinary piety and righteousness in their superstitious worship (Colossians 2:16-23). So they had a false, proud, and bitter zeal (Galatians 4:17-18); 1 Timothy 1:6 and 6:4-5). And likewise a false show of humility, in affecting an extraordinary outward meanness and dejection, when indeed they were 'vainly puffed up in their fleshly mind'; and made a righteousness of their humility, and were exceedingly lifted up with their eminent piety (Colossians 2:18, 23). But how do such things as these in the least injure those things that have been mentioned as the distinguishing evidences of the true Spirit? Besides such vain shows which may be from the devil, there are common influences of the Spirit, which are often mistaken for saving grace; but these are out of the question, because though they are not saving, they are still the work of the true Spirit.

Having thus fulfilled what I at first proposed, in considering what are the certain, distinguishing marks by which we may safely proceed in judging whether any work that falls under our observation is the work of the Spirit of God or not, I now proceed to the application.

The distinguishing marks of
a work of the Spirit of God:
Part 3

Practical inferences

The recent revival is from God

From what has been said, I will venture to draw this inference –
that the extraordinary influence that has lately appeared, causing
an uncommon concern and engagedness of mind about the things
of religion, is undoubtedly, in general, from the Spirit of God.

There are only two things that need to be known in order to
judge such a work, namely *facts* and *rules*. The *rules* of the word of
God we have had laid before us; and as to *facts*, there are only two
ways that we can come at them, so as to be in a capacity to compare
them with the rules, either by our own observation, or by informa-
tion from others who have had opportunity to observe them.

The facts of the case

As to this work, there are many things concerning it that are noto-
rious, and which, unless the apostle John was out in his rules, are
sufficient to determine it to be in general the work of God. The
Spirit that is at work takes off persons' minds from the vanities of
the world, and engages them in a deep concern about eternal happiness, and sets them earnestly seeking their salvation, and convinces
them of the dreadfulness of sin, and of their own guilty and miser-

able state as they are by nature. It awakens men's consciences, and makes them aware of the dreadfulness of God's anger, and causes in them a great desire and earnest care and endeavour to obtain his favour. It puts them upon a more diligent use of the means of grace which God has appointed; accompanied with a greater regard for the word of God, a desire of hearing and reading it, and of being more conversant with it than they used to be. And it is notoriously manifest that the spirit that is at work generally operates as a spirit of truth, making people more aware of their eternal salvation (e.g., that they must die, and that life is very short and uncertain; that there is a great sin-hating God, to whom they are accountable, and who will fix them in an eternal state in another world; and that they stand in great need of a Saviour). It makes people more aware of the value of Jesus who was crucified, and their need of him; and that it sets them earnestly seeking an interest in him. These things must be apparent to people in general throughout the land; for these things are not done in a corner; the work has not been confined to a few towns in some remoter parts, but has been carried on in many places all over the land, and in most of the principal, populous, and public places in it. Christ in this respect has wrought amongst us, in the same manner that he wrought his miracles in Judea. It has now been continued for a considerable time; so that there has been a great opportunity to observe the manner of the work. And all such as have been very conversant with the subjects of it see a great deal more that, by the rules of the apostle, clearly and certainly shows it to be the work of God.

A widespread work

And here I would observe that the nature and tendency of a spirit that is at work may be determined with much greater certainty, and less danger of being imposed upon, when it is observed in a great multitude of people of all sorts, and in various places, than when it is only seen in a few, in some particular place, that have been much conversant with one another. A few particular persons may agree to cheat others by a false pretence, and professing things of which they never were conscious. But the work is spread out over great parts of a country, in places distant from one another, among people of all sorts and of all ages, and in multitudes possessed of a sound mind, good understanding, and known integrity. All that is heard and seen in them can be observed for many months together, and by those who are most intimate with them in these affairs, and have long been acquainted with them. There would therefore be the greatest absurdity in supposing that it still cannot be determined what kind of influence the operation they are under has upon people's minds. Can it not be determined whether it tends to awaken their consciences, or to stupefy them; whether it inclines them more to seek their salvation, or neglect it; whether it seems to confirm them in a belief in the Scriptures, or to lead them to deism; whether it makes them have more regard for the great truths of religion, or less?

And here it is to be observed that for people to profess that they are so convinced of certain divine truths as to esteem and love them in a *saving manner*, and for them to profess that they are *more convinced* or confirmed in the truth of them than they used to be, and find that they have a greater regard for them than they had before, are two very different things. People of honesty and common sense have much greater right to demand credit to be given to the latter profession than to the former. Indeed in the former it is less likely that a people in general should be deceived than some particular individuals. But whether people's convictions, and the alteration in their dispositions and affections, are in a degree and manner that is saving is beside the present question. If there are such effects on people's judgements, dispositions, and affections, as have been spoken of, whether they are in a degree and manner that is saving or not, it is nevertheless a sign of the influence of the Spirit of God. Scripture rules serve to distinguish the common influences of the Spirit of God, as well as those that are saving, from the influences of other causes.

By the providence of God, I have for some months past been much amongst those who have been the subjects of the work in question; and particularly, have been in the way of seeing and observing those extraordinary things with which many people have been offended — such as people's crying out aloud, shrieking, being put into great agonies of body, etc. I have seen the manner and result of such operations, and the fruits of them, for several months together. Many of them were people with whom I have been intimately acquainted in soul concerns, before and since. So I look upon myself as called on this occasion to give my testimony that — so far as the nature and tendency of such a work is capable of falling under the observation of a bystander to whom those that have been the subjects of it have endeavoured to open their hearts, or can be come at by diligent and particular inquiry — this work has all those marks that have been pointed out. And this has been the case in very many instances, *every article*; and in many others, all those marks have appeared in a very *great degree*.

Two sorts of people

The subjects of these uncommon experiences have been of two sorts: either those who have been in great distress from an apprehension of their sin and misery; or those who have been overcome with a sweet sense of the greatness, wonderfulness, and excellency of divine things. Of the multitude of those of the former sort, that I have had opportunity to observe, there have been very few whose distress has not arisen apparently from real, proper conviction, and being in a degree conscious of that which was the truth. And though I do not suppose, when such things were observed to be common, that people have laid themselves under those violent restraints to avoid outward manifestations of their distress, that perhaps they otherwise would have done; yet there have been very few in whom there has been any appearance of feigning or affecting such manifestations, and very many for whom it would have been undoubtedly utterly impossible for them to avoid them. Generally, in these agonies they have appeared to be in the perfect exercise of their reason; and those of them who could speak have been well able to give an account of the circumstances of their mind, and the cause of their distress, at the time, and were able to remember and give an account of it afterwards.

I have known a very few instances of those who, in their great extremity, have for a short time been deprived in some measure of the use of reason; but among the many hundreds, and it may be thousands, that have recently been brought to such agonies, I never yet knew one lastingly deprived of their reason. Depression has evidently been part of the cause in some cases that I have known, and when it is so, the difference is very apparent; their distresses are of another kind, and operate in quite a different way from when their distress is from mere conviction. It is not only truth that distresses them, but many vain shadows and notions that will not yield either to Scripture or reason. Some in their great distress have not been well able to give an account of themselves, or to declare the cause of their trouble to others, yet I have had no reason to think they were not under proper convictions, and their state has ended up well. But this will not be at all wondered at by those who have had much to do with souls under spiritual difficulties: some things of which they are aware are altogether new to them; their ideas and inward sensations are new, and therefore they do not know how to express them in words. Some who, on first inquiry, said they did not know what was the matter with them have been able, on detailed examination and interrogation, to describe their case, though of themselves they could not find expressions and forms of speech to do it.

Some suppose that terrors producing such effects are only a fright. But certainly a distinction ought to be made between a very great fear, or extreme distress arising from an apprehension of some dreadful truth – a cause fully proportionable to such an effect – and a needless, causeless fright. The latter is of two kinds: either, first, when people are terrified with that which is not the truth (of which I have seen very few instances unless in cases of depression); or, secondly, when they are in a fright from some terrible outward appearance and noise, and a general notion arising from that. These people apprehend that there is something or other terrible, they know not what; without having in their minds any particular truth whatever. I have seen very little of this kind of fright among either old or young people.

Those who are suffering so much often express a great sense of their exceeding wickedness, the multitude and aggravations of their actual sins; their dreadful pollution, enmity, and perverseness; their obstinacy and hardness of heart; a sense of their great guilt in the sight of God; and the dreadfulness of the punishment which sin deserves. Very often they have a lively idea of the horrible pit of eternal misery; and at the same time it appears to them that the great God who has them in his hands is exceedingly angry, and his wrath appears amazingly terrible to them. God appears to them so much provoked, and his great wrath so increased, that they are apprehensive of great danger, and that he will not bear with them any longer but will now cut them off straight away, and send them down in the dreadful pit they have in view; and at the same time they see no refuge. They see more and more of the vanity of everything they used to trust to, and with which they flattered themselves, till they are brought wholly to despair of all, and to see that they are at the disposal of the mere will of that God who is so angry with them. Very many, in the midst of their extremity, have been brought to an extraordinary sense of their fully deserving that wrath, and the destruction which was then before their eyes. They feared every moment that it would be executed upon them; they have been greatly convinced that this would be altogether just, and that God is indeed absolutely sovereign. Very often, some text of Scripture expressing God's sovereignty has been brought home to their minds, and has calmed them. They have been brought, as it were, to lie at God's feet; and after great agonies, a little before light has arisen, they have been composed and quiet, in submission to a just and sovereign God; but their bodily strength much spent. Sometimes it looked as though their lives were almost gone; and the light has appeared, and a glorious Redeemer, with his wonderful, all-sufficient grace, has been represented to them often, in some sweet invitation of Scripture. Sometimes the light comes in suddenly, sometimes more gradually, filling their souls with love, admiration, joy, and self-abasement; drawing out their hearts after the excellent, lovely Redeemer, and longings to lie in the dust before him; and that others might see, embrace, and be delivered by him. They had longings to live to his glory; but were aware that they can do nothing of themselves, appearing vile in their own hearts. And all the appearances of a real change of heart have followed; and grace has acted, from time to time, in the same way that it used to act in those who were converted formerly, with similar difficulties, temptations, buffetings, and comforts; except that in many, the light and comfort have been greater than usual. Many very young children have been affected like this. There have been some instances very much like those we read of in Mark 1:26 and 9:26, where 'when the devil had cried with a loud voice, and rent them sore, he came out of them'. And probably those instances were intended as a type of such things as these. Some have several turns of great agonies before they are actually delivered; and others have been in such distress, which has passed off, and no deliverance at all has followed.

Confusion

Some people object that when a number together are making a noise in such circumstances, there is great confusion. They say that God cannot be the author of it because he is the God of order, not of confusion. But consider the proper meaning of confusion: it is breaking the order of things by which they are properly disposed, and duly directed to their end, so that the order and due connection of means is broken and they fail to achieve their end. Now the conviction of sinners for their conversion is achieving the end of religious means. Not but that I think the people thus extraordinarily moved should endeavour to refrain from such outward manifestations, as they well can do, and should refrain to their utmost at the time of their solemn worship. But if God chooses to convince people's consciences so that they cannot avoid great outward manifestations, even interrupting and breaking off those public means they were attending, I do not think this is confusion, or an unhappy interruption, any more than is a company met on the field to pray for rain, and were interrupted by a plentiful shower. Would to God that all the public assemblies in the land were interrupted with such confusion as this the next sabbath day! We need not be sorry for breaking the order of means by obtaining the end for which that order is made. He who is going to fetch a treasure need not be sorry that he is stopped by meeting the treasure on the way.

A sight of their own vileness

Besides those who are overcome with conviction and distress, I have seen many of late who have had their bodily strength taken away with a sense of the glorious excellence of the Redeemer, and the wonders of his dying love; with a very uncommon sense of their own littleness and exceeding vileness attending it, with all expressions and appearances of the greatest abasement and abhorrence of themselves. Not only new converts, but many who, we hope, were already converted, have had their love and joy attended with a flood of tears, and a great appearance of contrition and humiliation, especially for their having lived no more to God's glory since their conversion. These have had a far greater sight of their vileness, and the evil of their hearts, than ever they had; with an exceeding earnestness of desire to live better for the time to come, but attended with greater self-diffidence than ever; and many have been overcome with pity for the souls of others, and longing for their salvation.

I might mention many other things in this extraordinary work, answering to every one of those marks which have been insisted on. If the apostle John knew how to give signs of a work of the true Spirit, this is such a work.

Providence has cast my lot in a place where the work of God has *formerly* been carried on. I had the happiness to be settled in that place for two years with the venerable Stoddard; and was then acquainted with a number who, at that time, were wrought upon under his ministry, before that period, in a manner agreeable to the doctrine of all orthodox divines. And recently a work has been carried on there with very uncommon operations, but it is evidently the same work that was carried on there at other times, though attended with some new circumstances. And if this is not in general the work of God, we must certainly throw out all talk of conversion and Christian experience; and not only that, but we must throw out our Bibles, and give up revealed religion. Not that I suppose the degree of the Spirit's influence is to be determined by the degree of effect on people's bodies; or that the experiences which have the greatest influence on the body are always the best.

Irregularities

As for the imprudences, irregularities, and mixture of delusion that has been observed, it is not at all to be wondered at that a reformation, after a long-continued and almost universal deadness, should be accompanied by such things at first, when the revival is new. In the first creation God did not make a complete world at once, but there was a great deal of imperfection, darkness, and mixture of chaos and confusion after God first said, 'Let there be light,' before the whole stood forth in perfect form. When God at first began his great work for the deliverance of his people, after their long-continued bondage in Egypt, there were false wonders mixed with the true for a while; which hardened the unbelieving Egyptians, and made them doubt the divinity of the whole work. When the children of Israel first went to bring up the ark of God, after it had been neglected and had been long absent, they did not seek the Lord in the proper way (1 Chronicles 15:13). At the time when the sons of God came to present themselves before the Lord, Satan came among them too. And Solomon's ships, when they brought gold, silver, and pearls, also brought apes and peacocks. When daylight first appears after a night of darkness, we must expect to have darkness mixed with light for a while, and not have perfect day and the sun risen at once. The fruits of the earth are green at first, before they are ripe, and they come to their perfection gradually; and so, Christ tells us, is the kingdom of God. 'So is

65

the kingdom of God; as if a man should cast seed into the ground, and should sleep, and rise night and day; and the seed should spring and grow up, he knoweth not how: for the earth bringeth forth fruit of herself; first the blade, then the ear, after that the full corn in the ear' (Mark 4:26–28).

The imprudences and errors that have accompanied this work are the less to be wondered at when it is considered that chiefly young people have been the subjects of it, who have less steadiness and experience, and being in the heat of youth are much more ready to run to extremes. Satan will keep people secure as long as he can; but when he can do that no longer, he often endeavours to drive them to extremes, and so to dishonour God, and wound religion in that way. And doubtless it has been one occasion of much misconduct, that in many places people see plainly that their ministers have an ill opinion of the work; and therefore, with good reason, dare not go to them as their guides in it; and so are without guides. No wonder then that when a people are like sheep without a shepherd, they wander out of the way. A people in such circumstances stand in great and continual need of guides, and their guides are in continual need of much more wisdom than they have of their own. And if a people have ministers that favour the work, and rejoice in it, it is still not to be expected that either the people or ministers should know so well how to conduct themselves in such an extraordinary state of things – while it is new, and something they never had any experience of before, and time to see their tendency, consequences, and result. The happy influence of experience is very manifest at this day in the people among whom God has settled me to live. The work which has been carried on there this year has been much purer than what happened there six years earlier: it has seemed to be more purely spiritual, free from natural and corrupt mixtures, and anything savouring of enthusiastic wildness and extravagance. It has wrought more by deep humiliation and abasement before God and men; and they have been much freer from imprudences and irregularities. And particularly there has been a remarkable difference in this respect, that whereas many before, in their comforts and rejoicings, did too much forget their distance from God, and were ready in their conversation together of the things of God, and of their own experiences, to talk with too much lightness; but now they seem to have no disposition that way, but rejoice with a more solemn, reverential, humble joy, as God directs (Psalm 2:11). Not because the joy is not as great, and in many instances much greater. Many among us who were wrought upon in that earlier period have now had much greater communications from heaven than they had then. Their rejoicing operates in another manner; it abases them, breaks their hearts, and brings them into the dust. When they speak of their joys, it is not with laughter, but a flood of tears. Thus those who laughed before weep now, and yet by their united testimony, their joy is vastly purer and sweeter than that which before raised their animal spirits more. They are now more like Jacob, when God appeared to him at Bethel, when he saw the ladder that reached to heaven, and said, 'How dreadful is the place!' And like Moses, when God showed him his glory on the mount, when he made haste and 'bowed himself unto the earth'

We must not hinder the work

Let this warn us all not by any means to oppose the work, or do anything in the least to clog or hinder it; but, on the contrary, do our utmost to promote it.

Now Christ is come down from heaven in a remarkable and wonderful work of his Spirit, it becomes all his professed disciples to acknowledge him, and give him honour.

The example of the Jews

The example of the Jews in Christ's and the apostles' times is enough to make those who do not acknowledge this work very jealous of themselves, and to make them exceedingly cautious of what they say or do. Christ then was in the world, and the world did not receive him. That coming of Christ had been much spoken of in the prophecies of Scripture which they had in their hands, and it had been long expected; and yet because Christ came in a manner they did not expect, and which did not agree with their carnal reason, they would not own him. Indeed, they opposed him, counted him a madman, and pronounced the spirit by which he worked to be the spirit of the devil. They stood and wondered at the great things done, and knew not what to make of them; but they still met with so many stumbling-blocks that they finally could not acknowledge him. And when the Spirit of God came to be poured out so wonderfully in the apostles' days, they looked upon it as confusion and distraction. They were *astonished* by what they saw and heard, but not *convinced*. And especially was the work of God then rejected by those who were most conceited of their own understanding and knowledge, as Isaiah 29:14 said: 'Therefore, behold, I will proceed to do a marvellous work amongst this people, even a marvellous work and a wonder; for the wisdom of their wise men shall perish, and the understanding of their prudent men shall be hid.' And many who had had a reputation for religion and piety had a great spite against the work, because they saw it tended to diminish their honour, and to reproach their formality and luke-warmness. Some, upon these accounts, maliciously and openly opposed and reproached the work of the Spirit of God, and called it the work of the devil, against inward conviction, and so were guilty of the unpardonable sin against the Holy Spirit.

There is another, a spiritual coming of Christ, to set up his kingdom in the world, that is as much spoken of in Scripture prophecy as that first coming, and which has long been expected by the church of God. We have reason to think, from what is said of this, that it will be in many respects parallel with the other. And certainly that low state into which the visible church of God has lately been sunk is very parallel with the state of the Jewish church when Christ came; and it is therefore no wonder at all that when Christ comes his work should appear a strange work to most people; indeed, it would be a wonder if it were otherwise. Whether or not the present work is the beginning of that great and frequently predicted coming of Christ to set up his kingdom, it is evident from what has been said that it is a work of the same Spirit, and of the same nature. And there is no reason to doubt that the conduct of people who continue long to refuse to acknowledge Christ in the work – especially those who are teachers in his church – will be similarly provoking to God, as it was in the Jews of old, while refusing to acknowledge Christ; notwithstanding what they may plead of the great stumbling-blocks that are in the way, and the cause they have to doubt the work. The teachers of the Jewish church found innumerable stumbling-blocks that were insuperable to them. Many things appeared in Christ, and in the work of the Spirit after his ascension, which were exceedingly strange to them; they seemed assured that they had just cause for their scruples. Christ and his work were to the Jews a stumbling-block. 'But blessed is he,' says Christ, 'whosoever shall not be offended in me.' As strange and as unexpected as the manner of Christ's appearance was, yet he had not been long in Judaea working miracles before all those who had opportunity to observe, and yet refused to acknowledge him, brought fearful guilt upon themselves in the sight of God; and Christ condemned them, that though they could discern the face of the sky, and of the earth, yet they could not discern the signs of the times. 'Why,' he asks, 'even of yourselves, judge ye not what is right?' (Luke 12).

Silent ministers

It is not to be supposed that the great Jehovah has bowed the heavens and appeared here now for so long a time, in such a glorious work of his power and grace – in so extensive a manner, in the most public places of the land, and in almost all parts of it – without giving such evidences of his presence that great numbers and even many teachers in his church can remain guiltless in his sight, without ever receiving and acknowledging him, and giving him honour, and appearing to rejoice in his gracious presence; or without so much as once giving him thanks for so glorious and blessed a work of his grace, wherein his goodness does more appear than if he had bestowed on us all the temporal blessings that the world affords. A long-continued silence in such a case is undoubtedly provoking to God; especially in ministers. It is a secret kind of opposition that really tends to hinder the work. Such silent ministers stand in the way of the work of God, as Christ said of old, 'He that is not with us is against us.' Those who stand wondering at this strange work, not knowing what to make of it, and refusing to receive it – and ready it may be sometimes to speak contemptibly of it, as was the case with the Jews of old – would do well to consider, and to tremble at St Paul's words to them: 'Beware therefore lest that come upon you, which is spoken of in the prophets; Behold, ye despisers, and wonder, and perish: for I work a work in your days, which you shall in no wise believe, though a man declare it unto you' (Acts 13:40-41). Those who cannot believe the work to be true because of the extraordinary degree and manner of it should consider how it was with the unbelieving lord in Samaria, who said, 'Behold, if the Lord should make windows in heaven, might this thing be?' To whom Elisha said, 'Behold, thou shalt see it with thine eyes, but shalt not eat thereof.' Let all to whom this work is a cloud and darkness – as the pillar of cloud and fire was to the Egyptians – take heed that it be not their destruction, while it gives light to God's Israel.

I would entreat those who quiet themselves, that they proceed on a principle of prudence, and are waiting to see how things turn out – and what fruits those that are the subjects of this work will bring forth in their lives and conversations – to consider whether this will justify long refraining from acknowledging Christ when he appears so wonderfully and graciously present in the land. It is probably that many of those who are thus waiting do not know what they are waiting for. If they wait to see a work of God without difficulties and stumbling-blocks, it will be like the fool's waiting at the riverside to have the water all run by. A work of God without stumbling-blocks is never to be expected. 'It must need be that offences come' (Matthew 18:7). There never yet was any great manifestation that God made of himself to the world, without

70

many difficulties attending it. It is the same with God's works as it is with his word: they seem at first full of things that are strange, inconsistent, and difficult to the carnal unbelieving hearts of men. Christ and his work always was, and always will be, a stone of stumbling, and rock of offence, a gin and a snare to many. The prophet Hosea, speaking of a glorious revival of religion in God's church – when God would be as the dew unto Israel, who would grow as the lily, and put out roots like Lebanon, whose branches would spread, etc. – concludes: 'Who is wise, and he shall understand these things? prudent, and he shall know them? for the ways of the Lord are right, and the just shall walk in them: but the transgressors shall fail therein' (Hosea 14:9).

Stumbling-blocks to come

It is probable that the stumbling-blocks that now attend this work will in some respects be increased, and not diminished. We will probably see more instances of apostasy and gross iniquity among people who claim to be believers. And if one kind of stumbling-blocks are removed, it is to be expected that others will come. It is with Christ's works as it was with his parables; things that are difficult to men's dark minds are ordered purposely, to test their corrupt minds and spiritual sense; and so that those of corrupt minds and of an unbelieving, perverse, cavilling spirit, 'seeing might see and not understand'. Those who are now waiting to see how this work turns out think they will be better able to determine later on; but probably many of them are mistaken. The Jews that saw Christ's miracles waited to see better evidences of his being the Messiah; they wanted a sign from heaven; but they waited in vain; their stumbling-blocks did not diminish, but increased. They found no end to them, and so were more and more hardened in unbelief. Many have been praying for that glorious reformation spoken of in Scripture, and did not know what they have been praying for (as it was with the Jews when they prayed for the coming of Christ), and if it came they would not acknowledge or receive it.

This pretended prudence, in people waiting so long before they acknowledged this work, will probably in the end prove the greatest imprudence. Hereby they will fail to receive any share of so great a blessing, and will miss the most precious opportunity of obtaining divine light, grace, and comfort, heavenly and eternal benefits, that God ever gave in New England. While the glorious fountain is set open in so wonderful a manner, and multitudes flock to it and receive a rich supply for the needs of their souls, they stand at a distance, doubting, wondering, and receiving nothing, and are likely to continue thus till the precious season is past.

It is indeed to be wondered at that those who have doubted the work, which has been attended with such uncommon external appearances, should be easy in their doubts, without taking thorough pains to inform themselves, by going where such things have been to be seen, narrowly observing and diligently inquiring into them; not contenting themselves with observing two or three instances, nor resting till they were fully informed by their own observation. I do not doubt that if this course had been taken, it would have convinced all whose minds are not shut up against conviction. How greatly have they erred, when they have ventured to speak slightly of these things when they have only the uncertain reproofs of others! That caution of an unbelieving Jew might teach them more prudence: 'Refrain from these men, and let them alone; for if this counsel or this work be of men, it will come to nought; but if it be of God, ye cannot overthrow it; lest haply ye be found to fight against God' (Acts 5:38-39). Whether or not what has been said in this discourse is enough to produce conviction that this is the work of God, I hope that for the future they will at least listen to this caution of Gamaliel, so as not to oppose it, or say anything which has even an indirect tendency to bring it into discredit, lest they should be found opposers of the Holy Spirit. There is no kind of sin so hurtful and dangerous to the souls of men as those committed against the Holy Spirit. We had better speak against God the Father, or the Son, than to speak against the Holy Spirit in his gracious operations on the hearts of men. Nothing will so much tend for ever to prevent our having any benefit of his operations on our own souls.

If there are any who still resolutely go on to speak contemptibly of these things, I would beg them to take heed that they are not guilty of the unpardonable sin. When the Holy Spirit is much poured out, and men's lusts, lukewarmness, and hypocrisy are reproached by its powerful operations, then is the most likely time of any for this sin to be committed. If the work goes on, it is well if among the many that show an enmity against it, some are not guilty of this sin, if none have been already. Those who maliciously oppose and reproach this work, and call it the work of the devil, want but one thing of the unpardonable sin, and that is, doing it against inward conviction. And though some are so prudent as not openly to oppose and reproach this work, it is still to be feared – at this day, when the Lord is going forth so gloriously against his enemies – that many who are silent and inactive, especially ministers, will bring that curse of the angel of the Lord upon themselves: 'Curse ye Meroz, said the angel of the Lord, curse ye bitterly the inhabitants thereof; because they came not to the help of the Lord, to the help of the Lord against the mighty' (Judges 5:23).

A day of favour, a day of vengeance

Since the great God has come down from heaven, and manifested himself in so wonderful a manner in this land, it is vain for any of us to expect any other than to be greatly affected by it in our spiritual state and circumstances, respecting the favour of God, one way or another. Those who do not become more happy by it will become far more guilty and miserable. It is always so; such a season as proves an acceptable year, and a time of great favour to those who accept it and benefit from it, proves a day of vengeance to others (Isaiah 59:2). When God sends forth his *word*, it will not return to him void; much less his *Spirit*. When Christ was upon earth in Judaea, many people slighted and rejected him; but it proved in the end to be no matter of indifference to them. God made all that people to feel that Christ had been among them; those who did not

73

feel it to their comfort felt it to their great sorrow. When God only sent the prophet Ezekiel to the children of Israel, he declared that whether they would hear or whether they would forbear, they would still know that there had been a prophet among them. How much more may we suppose that when God has appeared so wonderfully in this land, he will make everyone know that the great Jehovah had been in New England.

We must give no excuse to those who reproach the work

In the last place, I now come to apply myself to those who are the friends of this work, who have been partakers of it, and are zealous to promote it. Let me earnestly exhort such people to give diligent heed to themselves to avoid all errors and misconduct, and whatever may darken and obscure the work; and to give no occasion to those who stand ready to reproach it. The apostle was careful to cut off occasion from those that desired occasion. The same apostle exhorts Titus to maintain a strict care and watch over himself, that both his preaching and behaviour might be such as could not be condemned; that he who was of the contrary part might be ashamed, having no evil thing to say of them (Titus 2:7-8). We need to be wise as serpents and harmless as doves. It is of no small consequence that we should at this day behave ourselves innocently and prudently. We must expect that the great enemy of this work will especially try his utmost with us; and he will especially triumph if he can prevail in anything to blind and mislead us. He knows it will do more to further his purpose and interest than if he prevailed against a hundred others. We need to watch and pray, for we are only little children; this roaring lion is too strong for us, and this old serpent too subtle for us.

Watch against pride

Humility and self-diffidence, and an entire dependence on our Lord Jesus Christ, will be our best defence. Let us therefore maintain the strictest watch against spiritual pride, or being lifted up with extraordinary experiences and comforts, and the high favours of heaven, that any of us may have received. We need after such favours to keep a specially strict and jealous eye upon our own hearts, lest there should arise self-exalting reflections upon what we have received, and high thoughts of ourselves as being some of the most eminent of saints and particular favourites of heaven, and that the secret of the Lord is specially with us. Let us not presume to think that we above all are fit to be advanced as the great instructors and censors of this evil generation; and, in a high conceit of our own wisdom and discerning, assume the airs of prophets, or extraordinary ambassadors of heaven. When great revelations of God are given to our souls, we should not shine bright in our own eyes. Moses, when he had been conversing with God in the mountain, though his face shone so as to dazzle the eyes of Aaron and the people, still did not shine in his own eyes; 'he wist not that his face shone'. Let no one think themselves out of danger of this spiritual pride, even in their best frames. God saw that the apostle Paul (though probably the most eminent saint that ever lived) was not out of danger of it, no, not when he had just been conversing with God in the third heaven: see 2 Corinthians 12:7. Pride is the worst viper in the heart; it is the first sin that ever entered into the universe, lies lowest of all in the foundation of the whole building of sin, and is the most secret, deceitful, and unsearchable in its ways of working, of any lust whatever. It is ready to mix with everything; and nothing is to hateful to God, contrary to the spirit of the gospel, or of so dangerous consequence; and there is no one sin that does so much let in the devil into the hearts of the saints, and expose them to his delusions. I have seen it in many instances, and that in eminent saints. The devil has come in at this door presently after some eminent experience and extraordinary communion with God, and has woefully deluded and led them astray, till God has mercifully opened their eyes and delivered them; and they themselves have afterwards been made aware that it was pride that betrayed them.

Impulses

Some of the true friends of the work of God's Spirit have erred in giving too much heed to impulses and strong impressions on their minds, as though they were messages direct from heaven to them of something that was to happen, or something that it was the mind and will of God that they should do, which was not signified or revealed anywhere in the Bible without those impulses. These impressions, if they are truly from the Spirit of God, are of a quite different nature from his gracious influences on the hearts of the saints: they are of the nature of the extraordinary gifts of the Spirit, and are properly inspiration, such as the prophets and apostles and others had of old; which the apostle distinguishes from the *grace* of the Spirit (1 Corinthians 13).

One reason why some people have been ready to lay weight on such impulses is an opinion they have had, that the glory of the approaching happy days of the church would partly consist in restoring those extraordinary gifts of the Spirit. This opinion, I believe, arises partly through lack of duly considering and comparing the nature and value of those two kinds of influences of the Spirit, namely those that are ordinary and gracious, and those that are extraordinary and miraculous. The former are by far the most excellent and glorious; as the apostle shows at length (1 Corinthians 12:31, etc.). Speaking of the extraordinary gifts of the Spirit, he says, 'But covet earnestly the best gifts; and yet I show you a more excellent way'; i.e. a more excellent way of the influence of the Spirit. And then he goes on, in the next chapter, to show what that more excellent way is – the grace of that Spirit, which summarily consists in charity, or divine love. And throughout that chapter he shows the great preference of that above inspiration. God communicates his own nature to the soul in saving grace in the heart, more than in all miraculous *gifts*. The blessed image of God consists in *that* and not in *these*. The excellence, happiness, and glory of the soul immediately consists in the former. That is a root which bears infinitely more excellent fruit. Salvation and the eternal enjoyment of God is promised to divine grace, but not to inspiration. A man may have those extraordinary gifts, and yet be abominable to God and go to hell. The spiritual and eternal life of the soul consists in the grace of the Spirit, which God bestows only on his favourites and dear children. He has sometimes thrown out the other as it were to dogs and swine, as he did to Balaam, Saul, and Judas; and some who, in the earliest times of the Christian church, committed the unpardonable sin (Hebrews 6). Many wicked men at the day of judgement will plead, 'Have we not prophesied in thy name, and in thy name cast out devils, and in thy name done many wonderful works?' The greatest privilege of the prophets and apostles was not their being inspired and working miracles, but their eminent holiness. The grace that was in their hearts was a thousand times more their dignity and honour than their miraculous gifts. The things in which we find David comforting himself are not his being a king, or a prophet, but the holy influences of the Spirit of God in his heart, communicating to him his divine light, love, and joy. The apostle Paul abounded in visions, revelations, and miraculous gifts, above all the apostles; but yet he esteems all things but loss for the excellence of the spiritual knowledge of Christ. It was not the gifts but the grace of the apostles that was the proper evidence of their names being written in heaven; in which Christ directs them to rejoice, much more than in the devils being subject to them. To have grace in the heart is a higher privilege than the blessed Virgin herself had, in having the body of the second person of the Trinity conceived in her womb, by the power of the Highest overshadowing her: 'And it came to pass as he spake these things, a certain woman of the company lift up her voice, and said unto him; Blessed is the womb that bare thee, and the paps that thou has sucked! But he said, Yea, rather blessed are they that hear the word of God and keep it' (Luke 11:27-28; see also Matthew (12:47ff.).

The influence of the Holy Spirit, or divine charity in the heart, is the greatest privilege and glory of the highest archangel in heaven; indeed this is the very thing by which the creature has fellowship with God himself, with the Father and the Son, in their beauty and happiness. By this the saints are made partakers of the divine nature, and have Christ's joy fulfilled in themselves.

The ordinary sanctifying influences of the Spirit of God are the *purpose* of all extraordinary gifts, as the apostle shows in Ephesians 4:11-13. They are good for nothing, any further than as they are subordinate to this end; they will be so far benefiting anyone without it, that they will only aggravate their misery. This is, as the apostle observes, the most excellent way of God's communicating his Spirit to his church; it is the greatest glory of the church in all ages. This glory is what makes the church on earth most like the church in heaven, when prophecy and tongues and other miraculous gifts cease. And God communicates his Spirit only in that more excellent way of which the apostle speaks, namely *charity*, or divine love, 'which never faileth'. Therefore the glory of the approaching happy state of the church does not at all require these extraordinary gifts. As that state of the church will be the nearest of any to its perfect state in heaven, so I believe it will be like it in this, that all extraordinary gifts will have ceased and vanished away; and all those stars, and the moon, with the reflected light they gave in the night, or in a dark season, will be swallowed up in the sun of divine love. The apostle speaks of these gifts of inspiration as childish things in comparison with the influence of the Spirit in divine love – things given to the church only to support it in its minority, till the church has a complete standing rule established, and all the ordinary means of grace are settled; but as things that would cease as the church advanced to the state of manhood. 'When I was a child, I spake as a child, I understood as a child, I thought as a child; but when I became a man, I put away childish things' (1 Corinthians 13:11 – compare the three preceding verses).

The maturity of the church

When the apostle, in this chapter, speaks of prophecies, tongues, and revelations ceasing, and vanishing away in the church – when the Christian church advances from a state of minority to a state of manhood – he seems to be referring to its coming to an adult state in this world, as well as in heaven; for he speaks of a state of manhood in which those three things, Faith, Hope, and Charity, remain after miracles and revelations had ceased; as in the last verse, and 'now abideth [remaineth] Faith, Hope, and Charity, these three'. The apostle's manner of speaking here shows an evident reference to what he had just been saying before; and here is a manifest *antithesis* between *remaining* and that *failing, ceasing*, and *vanishing* away spoken of in verse 8. The apostle had been showing how all those gifts of inspiration, which were the leading-strings of the Christian church in its infancy, would vanish away when the church came to a state of manhood. Then he returns to observe what things remain after those had failed and ceased; and he observes that those three things shall remain in the church, Faith, Hope, and Charity; and therefore the adult state of the church he speaks of is the more perfect one at which it will arrive on earth, especially in the latter ages of the world. And this was the more properly observed to the church at Corinth, upon two accounts: because the apostle had previously observed to that church that they were in a state of infancy (3:1-2), and because that church seems above all others to have abounded with miraculous gifts.

When the expected glorious state of the church comes, the increase of light will be so great that it will in some respects answer what is said in verse 12 of *seeing face to face*. (See Isaiah 24:23 and 25:7.)

Therefore I do not expect a restoration of these miraculous gifts in the approaching glorious times of the church, nor do I desire it. It appears to me that it would add nothing to the glory of those times, but rather diminish it. For my part, I would rather enjoy the sweet influences of the Spirit, showing Christ's spiritual divine beauty, infinite grace, and dying love, drawing out the holy exercise of faith, divine love, sweet complacence, and humble joy in God, one quarter of an hour, than to have prophetic visions and revelations the whole year. It appears to me much more probable that God should give immediate revelations to his saints in the dark times of prophecy than now in the approach of the most glorious and perfect state of his church on earth. It does not appear to me that there is any need of those extraordinary gifts to introduce this happy state, and set up the kingdom of God through the world; I have seen so much of the power of God in a more excellent way, as to convince me that God can easily do it without.

I would therefore entreat the people of God to be very cautious how they give heed to such things. I have seen them fail in very many instances, and know by experience that impressions made with great power, and on the minds of true and eminent saints – even in the midst of extraordinary exercises of grace, and sweet communion with God, and attended with texts of Scripture strongly impressed on the mind – are no sure signs of their being revelations from heaven. I have known such impressions fail, in some instances, attended with all these circumstances. Those who leave the sure word of prophecy – which God has given to us as a light shining in a dark place – to follow such impressions and impulses, leave the guidance of the polar star to follow a jack-o'-lantern. No wonder therefore that sometimes they are led into woeful extravagancies.

Human learning

Moreover, seeing inspiration is not to be expected, *let us not despise human learning*. Those who assert that human learning is of little or no use in the work of the ministry do not well consider what they say; if they did, they would not say it. By human learning I mean, and suppose others to mean, the use of common knowledge by human and outward means. And therefore, to say that human learning is of no use is as much as to say that the education of a child, or the common knowledge which a grown man has more than a little child, is of no use. At this rate, a child of four years old is as fit for a teacher in the church of God, with the same degree of grace – and capable of doing as much to advance the kingdom of Christ by his instruction – as a very knowing man of thirty years of age. If adult persons have greater ability and advantage to do service, because they have more knowledge than a little child, then doubtless if they have more human knowledge still, with the same degree of grace, they would have still greater ability and advantage to do service. An increase of knowledge, without doubt, increases a man's advantage either to do good or harm, according as he is disposed. It is too obvious to be denied that God made great use of human learning in the apostle Paul, as he also did in Moses and Solomon.

And if knowledge, obtained by human means, is not to be despised, then it will follow that the means of obtaining it are not to be neglected, namely *study*; and that this is of great use in order to prepare for public instruction of others. And though having the heart full of the powerful influences of the Spirit of God may at some time enable people to speak profitably, indeed most excellently, without study; yet this will not warrant us needlessly to cast ourselves down from the pinnacle of the temple, depending upon it that the angel of the Lord will bear us up, and keep us from dashing our foot against a stone, when there is another way to go down, though it may not be as quick. And I would pray that *method* in public discourses, which tends greatly to help both the understanding and memory, may not be wholly neglected.

Judging other Christians

Another thing I would beg the dear children of God to consider more fully is how far, and upon what grounds, the rules of the Holy Scriptures will truly justify their censuring other professing Christians as hypocrites and ignorant of real religion. We all know that there is a judging and censuring of some sort or other that the Scripture very often and very strictly forbids. Desire that those rules of Scripture may be looked into, and thoroughly weighed; and that it may be considered whether our taking it upon us to discern the state of others – and to pass sentence upon them as wicked men, though they are professing Christians, and of good behaviour – is not really forbidden by Christ in the New Testament. If it is, then doubtless the disciples of Christ ought to avoid this practice, however qualified they may think themselves for it; or however needful, or useful, they may think it. It is plain that the sort of judgement which God claims as his prerogative, whatever that is, is forbidden. We know that a certain judging of the hearts of the children of men is often spoken of as the great prerogative of God, and which belongs only to him; as in 1 Kings 8:39 – 'Forgive, and do, and give unto every man according to his ways, whose heart thou knowest; for thou, even thou only, knowest the hearts of all the children of men.' And if we examine, we shall find that the judging of hearts which is spoken of as God's prerogative relates not only the aims and suppositions of men's hearts in particular actions, but chiefly to the state of their hearts as the professors of religion, and with regard to that profession. This will appear very manifest by looking over the following scriptures: 1 Chronicles 28:9; Psalm 7:9–11; Psalm 26; Proverbs 16:2; 17:3; 21:2; Job 2:23–25; Revelation 2:22–23. The sort of judging which is God's own business is forbidden: 'Who art thou that judgest another man's servant? To his own master he standeth or falleth' (Romans 14:4). 'There is one lawgiver that is able to save or destroy; who art thou that judgest another?' (James 4:12). 'But with me it is a very small thing, that I should be judged of you, or of man's judgement; yea I judge not mine own self; but he that judgeth me is the Lord' (2 Corinthians 4:13–14).

Again, whatever kind of judging is the proper work and business of the day of judgement is what we are forbidden: 'Therefore judge nothing before the time, until the Lord come; who both will bring to light the hidden things of darkness, and will make manifest the counsels of the heart; and then shall every man have praise of God' (1 Corinthians 4:5). But to distinguish hypocrites from true saints, when they have the form of godliness and the behaviour of godly men – or to separate the sheep from the goats – is the proper business of the day of judgement. Indeed, it is represented as the main business and purpose of that day. Therefore people greatly err when they take it upon them positively to determine who are sincere and who are not – to draw the dividing line between true saints and hypocrites, and to separate between sheep and goats, setting the one on the right hand and the other on the left – and to distinguish and gather out the tares from amongst the wheat.

Many of the servants of the owner of the field are very ready to think themselves sufficient for this, and are forward to offer their service to this end; but their Lord Jesus says, 'Nay, lest while ye gather up the tares, ye root up also the wheat with them. Let both grow together until the harvest.' And in the time of harvest will take care to see a thorough separation made (Matthew 13:28–30). This is in keeping with the apostle's prohibition mentioned above:

'Judge nothing before the time' (1 Corinthians 4:5).

In this parable, the servants who have the care of the fruit of the field doubtless mean the same as the servants who have the care of the fruit of the vineyard (Luke 20), and who are elsewhere represented as servants of the Lord of the harvest, appointed as labourers in his harvest. These we know are ministers of the gospel. *Now* is that parable in Matthew 13 fulfilled: 'While men sleep,' (during a long, sleepy, dead time in the church) 'the enemy has sowed tares.' Now is the time 'when the blade is sprung up,' and religion is reviving; and now some of the servants who have the care of the field say, 'Let us go and gather up the tares.'

I know that men who suppose they have some experience of the power of religion are very apt to think themselves capable of discerning and determining the state of others by a little conversation with them; and experience has taught me that this is an error. I once did not imagine that the heart of man has been so unsearchable as it is. I am less charitable, and less uncharitable than once I was. I find more things in wicked men that may counterfeit, and make a fair show of piety; and more ways that the remaining corruption of the godly may make them appear like carnal men, formalists, and dead hypocrites, than once I knew of. The longer I live, the less I wonder that God challenges it as his prerogative to try the hearts of the children of men, and directs that this business should be let alone till harvest. I desire to adore the wisdom of God, and his goodness to me and my fellow-creatures, that he has not committed this great business into the hands of such a poor, weak, and dim-sighted creature – one of so much blindness, pride, partiality, prejudice, and deceitfulness of heart – but has committed it into the hands of one infinitely fitter for it, and has made it his prerogative.

The talk of some persons, and the account they give of their experiences, is exceedingly satisfying, and such as forbids and banishes the thought of their being any other than the precious children of God. It obliges, and as it were forces, full charity; but yet we must allow the Scriptures to stand good that speak of everything in the saint, belonging to the spiritual and divine life, as hidden (Colossians 3:3–4). Their food is the hidden manna; they have meat to eat that others know not of; a stranger does not intermeddle with their joys. The heart in which they possess their divine distinguishing ornaments is the hidden man, and in the sight of God only (1 Peter 3:4). Their new name, which Christ has given them, no man knows but he that receives it (Revelation 2:17). The praise of the true Israelites, whose circumcision is that of the heart, is not of men but of God (Romans 2:29); that is, they can be certainly known and discerned to be Israelites, so as to have the honour that belong to such, only by God; as appears from the use of the same expression by the same apostle in 1 Corinthians 4:5. Here he speaks of its being God's prerogative to judge who are upright Christians, and what he will do at the day of judgement, adding, 'and then shall every man have praise of God'.

The instance of *Judas* is remarkable. Though he had been so much amongst the rest of the disciples, all persons of true experience, but his associates never seem to have entertained a thought of his being any other than a true disciple, till he revealed himself by his scandalous practice.

And the instance of *Ahitophel* is also very remarkable. David did not suspect him, though he was so wise and holy a man, so great a divine, and had such a great acquaintance with Scripture. He knew more than all his teachers, more than the ancients; he had grown old in experience, and was in the greatest ripeness of his judgement. He was a great prophet, and was intimately acquainted with Ahitophel, being his familiar friend, and most intimate companion in religious and spiritual concerns. Yet David not only never discovered him to be a hypocrite, but relied on him as a true saint. He relished his religious discourse, it was sweet to him, and he counted him an eminent saint; so that he made him above any man his guide and counsellor in soul matters; but yet he was not only no saint, but a notoriously wicked man, a murderous, vile wretch. 'Wickedness is in the midst thereof; deceit and guile depart not from her streets: for it was not an open enemy that reproached me, then I could have borne it; neither was it he that hated me, that did magnify himself against me, then I would have hid myself from him: but it was thou, a man mine equal, my guide and mine acquaintance: we took sweet counsel together, and walked unto the house of God in company' (Psalm 55:11–14).

To suppose that men have ability and right to determine the state of the souls of visible Christians, and so to make an open separation between saints and hypocrites, that true saints may be of one visible company, and hypocrites of another, separated by a partition that men make, carries in it an inconsistency, for it supposes that God has given men power to make another visible church, within his visible church; for by visible Christians or visible saints is meant people who have a right to be received as such in the eye of public charity. None can have a right to exclude any one of this visible church except in the way of that regular ecclesiastical proceeding which God has established in his visible church.

I beg those who have a true zeal for promoting this work of God to consider these things carefully. I am persuaded that whichever of them have much to do with souls, if they do not listen to me now, they will be of the same mind when they have had more experience.

Persecution

And another thing that I would entreat the zealous friends of this glorious work of God to avoid, is managing the controversy with opposers with too much heat, and appearance of an angry zeal; and particularly insisting very much in public prayer and preaching, on the persecution of opposers. If their persecution were ten times as great as it is, I think it would not be best to say so much about it. If it becomes Christians to be like lambs, not apt to complain and cry when they are hurt, it becomes them to be dumb and not to open their mouth, after the example of our dear Redeemer; and not to be like swine, that are apt to scream aloud when they are touched. We should not be ready to think and speak straightaway of fire from heaven, when the Samaritans oppose us and will not receive us into their villages. God's zealous ministers would do well to think of the direction the apostle Paul gave to a zealous minister: 'And the servant of the Lord must not strive, but be gentle unto all men, apt to teach, patient, in meekness instructing those that oppose themselves; if God peradventure will give them repentance, to the acknowledging of the truth; and that they may recover themselves out of the snare of the devil, who are taken captive by him at his will' (2 Timothy 2:24-26).

I would humbly recommend to those that love the Lord Jesus Christ, and would advance his kingdom, to follow that excellent rule of prudence which Christ has left us: 'No man putteth a piece of new cloth into an old garment; for that which is put in to fill it up, taketh from the garment, and the rent is made worse. Neither do men put new wine into old bottles; else the bottles break and the wine runneth out, and the bottles perish. But they put new wine into new bottles, and both are preserved' (Matthew 9:16-17). I am afraid the wine is now running out in some parts of this land, for lack of attendance to this rule. For though I believe we have confined ourselves too much to a certain stated method and form in the management of our religious affairs; which has had a tendency to cause all our religion to degenerate into mere formality; yet whatever has the appearance of a great innovation – that tends much to shock and surprise people's minds, and to set them talking and disputing – tends greatly to hinder the progress of the power of religion. It raises the opposition of some, diverts the minds of others, and perplexes many with doubts and scruples. It causes people to swerve from their great business, and turn aside to vain jangling. Therefore that which is very much beside the common practice had better be avoided, unless it is of considerable importance in its own nature. In this we shall follow the example of one who had the greatest success in propagating the power of religion: 'Unto the Jews I became as a Jew, that I might gain the Jews; to them that are under the law, as under the law, that I might gain them that are under the law; to them that are without law, as without law, (being without law to God, but under to Christ,) that I might gain them that are without law. To the weak I became as weak, that I might gain the weak. I am made all things to all men, that I might by all means save some. And this I do for the gospel's sake, that I might be partaker thereof with you' (1 Corinthians 9:20-23).

Christian charity *or*, The duty of charity to the poor, explained and enforced

If there be among you a poor man of one of thy brethren within any of thy gates in thy land which the Lord thy God giveth thee, thou shalt not harden thine heart, nor shut thine hand from thy poor brother: but thou shalt open thine hand unto him, and shalt surely lend him sufficient for his need, in that which he wanteth. Beware that there be not a thought in thy wicked heart, saying, The seventh year, the year of release, is at hand; and thine eye be evil against thy poor brother, and thou givest him nought; and he cry unto the Lord against thee, and it be sin unto thee. Thou shalt surely give him, and thine heart shall not be grieved when thou givest unto him: because that for this thing the Lord thy God shall bless thee in all thy works, and in all that thou puttest thine hand unto. For the poor shall never cease out of the land: therefore I command thee, saying, Thou shalt open thine hand wide unto thy brother, to thy poor, and to thy needy, in thy land. (Deuteronomy 15:7–11)

The words explained

The duty enjoined here is giving to the poor: 'If there be among you a poor man of one of thy brethren . . . thou shalt not harden thine heart, nor shut thine hand' from thy poor brother: thou shalt surely give him. Here by *thy poor brother* is to be understood the

87

same as in other places is meant by *neighbour*. It is explained in Leviticus 25:35 to mean not only those of their own nation, but even strangers and sojourners: 'And if thy brother be waxen poor, and fallen in decay with thee; then thou shalt relieve him: yea though he be a *stranger*, or a *sojourner*.' The Pharisees indeed interpreted it to signify only one of their own nation; but Christ condemns this interpretation (Luke 10:29ff.), and teaches, in contradiction to their opinion, that the rules of charity in the law of Moses are to be extended to the Samaritans, who were not of their nation, and between whom and the Jews there was the most bitter enmity, and who were a people very troublesome to the Jews.

God gives us directions *how* we are to give in such a case, namely *bountifully* and *willingly*. We should give *bountifully*, and *sufficiently* for the supply of the poor's need: 'Thou shalt not shut up thine hand from thy poor brother; but thou shalt open thine hand wide unto him, and lend him sufficient for his need, in that which he wanteth' (verse 7). And again: 'Thou shalt open thine hand wide unto thy brother, to thy poor, and to thy needy, in thy land' (verse 11). Again, we should give *willingly* and without grudging: 'Thou shalt not harden thine heart from thy poor brother' (verse 7). 'And thine heart shall not be grieved when thou givest him' (verse 10).

We may also observe how peremptorily this duty is here enjoined, and how much it is insisted on. It is repeated over and over again, and enjoined in the strongest terms: 'Thou shalt not harden thine heart, nor shut thine hand from thy poor brother' (verse 7). 'But thou shalt open thine hand wide unto him' (verse 8). 'Thou shalt surely give him' (verse 10). 'I command thee, saying Thou shalt open thine hand wide unto thy brother, to thy poor, and to thy needy' (verse 11).

Moreover, God strictly warns against objections. 'Beware that there be not a thought in thy wicked heart, saying, The seventh year, the year of release, is at hand; and thine eye be evil against thy poor brother, and thou give him nought, and he cry unto the Lord against thee, and it be sin unto thee' (verse 9). The matter concerning the seventh year, or year of release, was thus: God had given Israel a law that every seventh year should be a year of release: if any man had lent anything to any of his poor neighbours, if the latter had not been able to repay it before that year, the former should release it, and should not exact it of his neighbour, but give it to him. Therefore God warns the children of Israel against making this an objection to helping their poor neighbours, that the year of release was near at hand; and it was not likely that they would be able to refund it again before that time, and then they would lost it wholly, because then they would be obliged to release it. God foresaw that the wickedness of their hearts would be very ready to make such an objection; but very strictly warns them against it, that they should not be the more backward to supply the wants of the needy for that, but should be willing to give him: 'Thou shalt be willing to lend, expecting nothing again'.

Men are exceedingly apt to make objections against such duties as God speaks of here, as a manifestation of the wickedness of their hearts: 'Beware that there be not a thought in thy wicked heart . . .' The warning is very strict. God not only says, Beware that thou do not actually refuse to give him, but, Beware that thou have not one objecting thought against it, arising from a backwardness to liber- ality. God warns against the beginnings of uncharitableness in the heart, and against whatever tends to a reluctance to give: 'And thou give him nought, and he cry unto the Lord against thee, and it be sin unto thee'. God warns them from the guilt which they would be liable to bring themselves in this way.

We may observe here several *enforcements* of this duty. There is a reason of this duty implied in God's calling the needy person our brother: 'Thou shalt not . . . shut thine hand from thy poor brother' (verse 7). 'Beware that thine eye be not evil against thy poor brother' (verse 9). 'Thou shalt open thine hand wide to thy brother' (verse 11). We are to look upon ourselves as related to all mankind, but especially to those who are of the visible people of God. We are to look upon them as brothers, and to treat them accordingly. We are base indeed if we are not willing to help a *brother* in need.

Another enforcement of this duty is the promise of God that for this thing he will bless us in all our works, and in all that we put our hands to – a promise that we shall not lose, but gain by it (verse 10).

Another is that we shall never lack proper objects of our charity and bounty: 'For the poor shall never cease out of thy land' (verse 10). This God says to the Jewish Church; and Christ says the same to the Christian church: 'The poor ye have always with you' (Matthew 26:11). This is to cut off an excuse that uncharitable people would be ready to make for not giving, that they could find nobody to give to, that they saw none who were in need. God cuts off such an excuse by telling us that he would so order it in his providence that his people everywhere, and in all ages, will have occasion for the exercise of that virtue.

From this account the doctrine is obvious, that it is the absolute and indispensable duty of the people of God to give bountifully and willingly for supplying the wants of the needy. In particular:

We must give bountifully

It is the duty of the people of God to give *bountifully* for this purpose. It is commanded once and again in the text: 'Thou shalt open thine hand wide unto thy poor brother'. Merely to give something is not sufficient; it does not answer the rule, nor come up to the holy command of God; but we must open our hand wide. What we give, considering our neighbour's wants, and our ability, should be such as may be called a *liberal* gift. What is meant in the text by opening the hand wide, with respect to those that are able, is explained in verse 8: 'Thou shalt open thine hand wide unto him, and shalt surely lend him sufficient for his want, in that which he needeth'. By lending here, as is evident from the two following verses, and as we have just now shown, is not only meant lending to receive again; the word *lend* in Scripture is sometimes used for giving, as in Luke 6:35: 'Do good and lend, hoping for nothing again.'

We are commanded, therefore, to give our poor neighbour what is sufficient for his need. No one ought to be allowed to live in pinching want among a visible people of God, who are able: except in case of idleness, or prodigality, or some such case which the word of God excepts. It is said that the children of Israel should lend to the poor, and in the year of release should release what they had lent, *save when there should be no poor among them*. It is rendered in the margin, *to the end there be no poor among you*; i.e. you should so supply the wants of the needy that there may be none among you in pinching want. This translation seems the more likely to be the true one, because God says that there will be no time when there will be no poor who are proper objects of charity (verse 11).

When people give very *sparingly*, it is no manifestation of charity, but of a contrary spirit. 'Therefore I thought it necessary to exhort the brethren, that they would go before unto you, and make up beforehand your bounty, whereof ye had notice before, that the same might be ready, as a matter of bounty, and not as of covetousness' (2 Corinthians 9:5). The apostle here calls a very sparing contribution a matter of covetousness.

We must give freely

It is the duty of the visible people of God to give for the supply of the need *freely* and without grudging. It does not at all answer the rule in the sight of God if it is done with an inward grudging, or if the heart is grieved, and it inwardly hurts the man to give what he gives: 'Thou shalt surely give,' says God, 'and thine heart shall not be grieved.' God looks at the heart and the hand is not accepted without it: 'Every man according as he hath purposed in his heart, so let him give, not grudgingly, or of necessity; for God loveth a cheerful giver' (2 Corinthians 9:7).

We are obliged to give

This is a duty to which God's people are under very strict *obligations*. It is not merely a commendable thing for a man to be kind and bountiful to the poor, but our bounden duty, as much a duty as it is to pray, or to attend public worship, or anything else whatever; and the neglect of it brings great guilt upon any person.

The obligation of Christians to perform the duty of charity to the poor

It is mentioned in Scripture not only as a duty but a great duty. Indeed it is generally acknowledged to be a duty to be kind to the needy; but by many people it seems not to be looked upon as a duty of great importance. However, it is mentioned in Scripture as one of the greater and more essential duties of religion: 'He hath showed thee, O man, what is good; and what doth the Lord thy God require of thee, but to do justly, *to love mercy*, and to walk humbly with thy God? (Micah 6:8). Here to *love* mercy is mentioned as one of the three great things that are the sum of all religion. So it is mentioned by the apostle James as one of the two things wherein pure and undefiled religion consists: 'Pure religion, and undefiled, before God and the Father, is this, To visit the fatherless and widows in their affliction, and to keep himself unspotted from the world.' (James 1:27).

Similarly, Christ tells us it is one of the weightier matters of the law: 'Ye have omitted the weightier matters of the law, judgment, mercy, and faith' (Matthew 22:23). The Scriptures again and again teach us that it is a more weighty and essential thing than attending on the outward ordinances of worship: 'I desired mercy, and not sacrifice' (Hosea 6:6; see also Matthew 9:13 and 12:7). I know of scarcely any duty which is so much insisted on, so pressed and urged upon us, both in the Old Testament and the New, as this duty of charity to the poor.

The reason of the thing strongly obliges to it. It is not only very positively and frequently insisted on by God, but is most reasonable in itself; and so, on this account, there is reason why God should much insist upon it.

The state of mankind

It is most reasonable considering the general state and nature of mankind. This makes it most reasonable that we should love our neighbour as ourselves, for men are made in the image of our God, and on this account are worthy of our love. Besides, we are all closely allied to one another by nature. We all have the same nature, similar faculties, similar dispositions, similar desires of good, similar needs, similar aversion to misery, and are made of one blood; and we are made to subsist by society and union with one another. God has made us with such a nature that we cannot subsist without the help of one another. Mankind in this respect are like the parts of the body – one cannot subsist alone, without being joined to and helped by the rest.

Now, this state of mankind shows how reasonable and suitable it is that men should love their neighbours; and that we should not look everyone at his own things, but every man also at the things of others (Philippians 2:4). A selfish spirit is very unsuitable to the nature state of mankind. He who is all for himself, and not for his neighbours, deserves to be cut off from the benefit of human society, and to be turned out among wild beasts, to subsist by himself as well as he can. A private niggardly spirit is more suitable for wolves, and other beasts of prey, than for human beings.

To love our neighbour as ourselves is the sum of the moral law respecting our fellow-creatures; and to help them, and to contribute to their relief, is the most natural expression of this love. It is vain to pretend to a spirit of love to our neighbours when it is grievous to us to part with anything for their help, when in calamity. Those who love only in word, and in tongue, and not in deed, have no love in truth. Any profession without it is a vain pretence. To refuse to give to the needy is unreasonable, because in doing so we do to others contrary to what we would have others do to us in similar circumstances. We are very conscious of our own calamities, and when we suffer, are ready enough to think that our state requires the compassion and help of others; and are ready enough to think it hard if others will not deny themselves in order to help us when in straits.

Our circumstances under the gospel

It is especially reasonable considering our circumstances, under such a dispensation of grace as that of the gospel. Consider how much God has done for us, how greatly he has loved us, what he has given us, when we were so unworthy, and when his happiness could not be increased by us. Consider that silver, and gold, and earthly crowns, were in his esteem only mean things to give us, and he has therefore given us his own Son. Christ loved and pitied us when we were poor, and he spent himself to help, and even shed his own blood for us without grudging. He did not think much to deny himself, and to be at great cost for us vile wretches, in order to make us rich, and to clothe us with kingly robes, when we were naked; to feast us at his own table with infinitely costly dainties when we were starving; to advance us from the dunghill, and set us among princes, and make us inherit the throne of his glory, and so to give us the enjoyment of the greatest wealth and plenty to all eternity. 'For ye know the grace of our Lord Jesus Christ, that though he was rich, yet for your sakes he became poor, that ye through his poverty might be rich' (2 Corinthians 8:9).

Considering all these things, what a poor business it will be if those who hope to share these benefits cannot give something for the relief of a poor neighbour without grudging! That it should grieve them to part with a small matter to help a fellow servant in calamity, when Christ did not grudge to shed his own blood for them!

How unsuitable it is for us, who live only by kindness, to be unkind! What would have become of us, if Christ had been so sparing with his blood, and loth to bestow it, as many men are with their money and goods? Or if he had been as ready to excuse himself from dying for us as men commonly are to excuse themselves from charity to their neighbour? If Christ had made such objections as men commonly do in performing deeds of charity to their neighbour, he would have found enough of them.

Besides, Christ, by his redemption, has brought us into a closer relation to one another, has made us children of God, children in the same family. We are all brothers, having God for our common Father; which is much more than to be brothers in any other family. He has made us all one body; therefore we ought to be united, and subserve one another's good, and bear one another's burdens, as is the case with the parts of the same body. If one of the members suffer, all the others bear the burden with it (1 Corinthians 12:26). If one part is diseased or wounded, the others will minister to it and help it. Surely it should be the same in the body of Christ: 'Bear ye one another's burdens, and so fulfil the law of Christ' (Galatians 6:2).

Apply these things to yourselves; and inquire whether you do not lie under guilt on account of the neglect of this duty, in withholding that charity which God requires of you towards the needy? You have often examined yourselves to see if you do not live in some way displeasing to God. Perhaps at such times it never came into your minds to ask whether you do not lie under guilt on this account. But this neglect certainly brings guilt upon the soul in the sight of God, as is evident from the text: 'Beware that thine eye be not evil against thy poor brother, and thou givest him nought, and he cry unto the Lord against thee, and it be sin unto thee' (verse 9). This is often mentioned as one of the sins of Judah and Jerusalem for which God was about to bring such terrible judgements upon them; and it was one of the sins of Sodom, for which that city was destroyed, that she did not give to supply the poor and needy: 'This was the iniquity of thy sister Sodom, pride, fullness of bread, and abundance of idleness in her, and in her daughters; neither did she strengthen the hand of the poor and needy' (Ezekiel 16:49).

And have we not reason to fear that much guilt lies upon this land on this very account? We have a high opinion of ourselves for religion; but do not many other countries shame us? Do the Roman Catholics not shame us in this respect? So far as I can understand the tenor of the Christian religion, and the rules of the word of God, these things are in no measure answered in this respect by the general practice of most people in this land. There are many who make a high profession of religion; but do not many of them need to be informed by the apostle James what true religion is?

Let everyone examine himself, whether he do not lie under guilt in this matter. Have you not forborne to give, when you have seen your brother in need? Have you not shut up the bowels of your compassion towards him, and forborne to deny yourselves a little for his relief? Or when you have given, have you not done it grudgingly? And has it not inwardly hurt and grieved you? You have looked upon what you have given as lost, so that what you have given has been, as the apostle expresses it, a matter of covetousness, rather than of bounty. Have not occasions of giving been unwelcome to you? Have you not been uneasy under them? Have you not felt a considerable reluctance to give? Have you not, from a grudging, backward spirit, been apt to raise objections against giving, and to excuse yourselves? Such things as these bring guilt upon the soul, and often bring down the curse of God upon the persons in whom these things are found, as we will go on to show.

An exhortation to the duty of charity to the poor

We claim to be Christians, we pretend to be the followers of Jesus, and to make the gospel our rule. We have the Bible in our houses. Let us not behave in this matter as if we had never seen the Bible, as if we were ignorant of Christianity, and did not know what kind of religion it is. How will it help to pretend to be Christians and at the same time to live in the neglect of those rules of Christianity which are mainly insisted upon in it? But there are several things which I would here propose for your consideration.

What you have is not your own

Consider that what you have is not your own; i.e. you have only a subordinate right. Your goods are only lent to you by God, to be used by you in such ways as he directs. You yourselves are not your own. 'Ye are not your own, for ye are bought with a price; your body and your spirit are God's' (1 Corinthians 6:20). And if you yourselves are not your own, so then neither are your possessions your own. Many of you have by covenant given up yourselves and all you have to God. You have disowned and renounced any right in yourselves or in anything that you have, and have given to God all the absolute right; and if you are true Christians, you have done it from the heart.

Your money and your goods are not your own; they are only committed to you as stewards, to be used for him who committed them to you. 'Use hospitality one to another without grudging. As every man hath received the gift, even so minister the same one to another, as good stewards of the manifold grace of God' (1 Peter 4:9–10). A steward has no business with his master's goods, to use them in any other way than for the benefit of his master and his family, or according to his master's direction. He has no business to use them as if he were the proprietor of them; he has nothing to do with them except as he is to use them for his master. He is to give every one of his master's family their portion of meat in due season.

But if instead of that he hoards up his master's goods for himself, and withholds them from those of the household, so that some of the family are pinched for want of food and clothing, he is guilty of robbing his master and embezzling his substance. And would any householder endure such a steward? If he discovered him in such a practice, would he not take his goods out of his hands and commit them to the care of some other steward, who would give every one of his family his portion of meat in due season? Remember that all of us must give account of our stewardship, and how we have disposed of those goods which our Master has put into our hands. And if when our Master comes to reckon with us, it is found that we have denied some of his family their proper provision, while we have hoarded up for ourselves, as if we had been the proprietors of our Master's goods, what account shall we give of this?

What we do to our neighbours is done to God

God tells us that he will look upon what is done in charity to our needy neighbours as done to him; and what is denied to them, as denied to him. 'He that hath pity on the poor lendeth to the Lord'

(Proverbs 19:17). God has chosen to make our needy neighbours his receivers. He in his infinite mercy has so interested himself in their case that he looks upon what is given in charity to them as given to himself. When we deny them what their circumstances require of us, he regards us as robbing him of his right.

Christ teaches us that we are to look upon our fellow Christians in this case as himself, and that our giving or withholding from them will be taken as if we behaved like that towards him: see Matthew 25:40, where Christ says to the righteous on his right hand, who had supplied the wants of the needy, 'In that ye have done it to one of the least of these my brethren, ye have done it unto me'. In the same way he says to the wicked who had not shown mercy to the poor, 'Inasmuch as ye did it not unto one of the least of these, ye did it not to me' (verse 45).

Now what stronger enforcement of this duty can be conceived, or is possible, than this, that Jesus Christ looks upon our kind and bountiful, or unkind and uncharitable, treatment of our needy neighbours as such a treatment of himself?

If Christ were upon earth, and dwelt among us in a frail body, as he once did, and were in calamitous and needy circumstances, would we not be willing to supply him? Would we be apt to excuse ourselves from helping him? Would we not be willing to supply him so that he might live free from distressing poverty? And if we did otherwise, would we not bring great guilt upon ourselves? And might not our conduct justly be very highly resented by God? Christ was once here in a frail body, stood in need of the charity, and was maintained by it: 'And certain women which had been healed of evil spirits and infirmities, Mary called Magdalen, out of whom went seven devils, and Joanna the wife of Chuza, Herod's steward, and Susanna, and many others, which ministered unto him of their substance' (Luke 8:2–3). Similarly, in many of his members, he still needs the charity of others.

We need to comply with the difficult duties of religion

Consider that there is an absolute necessity of our complying with the difficult duties of religion. To give to the poor in the manner and measure that the gospel prescribes is a difficult duty, i.e. it is very contrary to corrupt nature, to that covetousness and selfishness of which there is so much in the wicked heart of man. Man is naturally governed only by a principle of self-love; and it is a difficult thing to corrupt nature for men to deny themselves of their present interest, trusting in God to make it up to them afterwards. But how often Christ has told us of the necessity of doing difficult duties of religion if we want to be his disciples – that we must sell all, take up our cross daily, deny ourselves, renounce our worldly profits and interests, etc. And if this duty seems hard and difficult to you, do not let that be an objection against your doing it; for you have got quite a wrong notion of things if you expect to go to heaven without performing difficult duties; if you expect any other than to find the way to life a narrow way.

This particular duty is necessary

The Scripture teaches us that this very particular duty is necessary. Particularly:

God will treat us as we treat others

The Scripture teaches that God will deal with us as we deal with our fellow creatures in this particular, and that with whatever measure we give to others in this respect, God will measure back to us. The Scriptures asserts this in both ways: it asserts that if we are of a merciful spirit, God will be merciful to us: 'Blessed are the merciful, for they shall obtain mercy' (Matthew 5:7). 'With the merciful thou wilt show thyself merciful' (Psalm 18:25). On the other hand it tells us that if we are not merciful, God will not be merciful to us; and that all our pretences to faith and a work of conversion will not help us obtain mercy unless we are merciful to those who are in need. 'For he shall have judgment without mercy, that hath showed no mercy. –

What doth it profit, my brethren, though a man say he hath faith, and have not works? Can faith save him? If a brother or sister be naked, and destitute of daily food; and one of you say unto them, depart in peace, be you warmed, and filled; notwithstanding ye give them not those things which are needful to the body; what doth it profit?' (James 2:13-16).

An essential part of the godly character

This very thing is often mentioned in Scripture as an essential part of the character of a godly man. 'The righteous showeth mercy, and giveth . . . He is ever merciful, and lendeth' (Psalm 37:21, 26). 'A good man showeth favour, and lendeth . . . He hath dispersed, and given to the poor' (Psalm 112:5, 9). 'He that honoureth God, hath mercy on the poor' (Proverbs 14:31; see also Proverbs 21:26 and Isaiah 57:1). A *righteous* man and a *merciful* man are used as synonymous terms: 'The *righteous* perisheth, and *merciful* men are taken away.'

It is mentioned in the New Testament as a thing so essential that the contrary cannot consist without a *sincere* love to God. 'But whoso hath this world's goods, and seeth his brother have need, and shutteth up his bowels of compassion from him, how dwelleth the love of God in him? My little children let us not love in word, neither in tongue, but in deed and in truth. And hereby we know that we are of the truth, and shall assure our hearts before him' (1 John 3:17–19). Similarly the apostle Paul, when he writes to the Corinthians, and proposes their contributing for the supply of the poor saints, tells them what he does it for, namely, a test of their sincerity: 'I speak to prove the sincerity of your love' (2 Corinthians 8:8).

Men will be judged by this

Christ teaches that judgement will be passed at the great day according to men's works in this respect. This is taught us by Christ in the most particular account of the proceedings of that day that we have in the whole Bible (Matthew 25:34ff.). It is evident that Christ thus represented the proceedings and determinations of this great day as turning upon this one point, purposely, in order to lead us to this idea, and to fix it in us, that a charitable spirit and practice towards our brothers is necessary to salvation.

We will not be the losers by our charity

Consider what abundant encouragement the word of God gives, that you will be no losers by your charity and bounty to those who are in want. As there is scarcely any duty prescribed in the word of God which is so much insisted on as this, so there is scarcely any to which there are so many promises of reward made. This virtue especially has the promises of this life and that which is to come. If we believe the Scriptures, when a man gives charitably to his neighbour in need, the giver has the greatest advantage by it, even greater than the receiver: 'I have showed you all things, how that so labouring ye ought to support the weak, and to remember the words of the Lord Jesus, how he said, It is more blessed to give than to receive' (Acts 20:35). The person who gives bountifully is a happier man than the one who receives bountifully: 'He that hath mercy on the poor, happy is he' (Proverbs 14:21).

Many people are ready to look on what is given for charitable uses as lost. But we ought not to look on it as lost, because it benefits those we ought to love as ourselves. And not only so, but it is not lost *to us*, if we give any credit to the Scriptures. See the advice that Solomon gave: 'Cast thy bread upon the waters, for thou shalt find it after many days' (Ecclesiastes 11:1). By casting our bread upon the waters, Solomon means giving it to the poor, as appears from the next words: 'Give a portion to seven, and also to eight'. Waters sometimes means people or multitudes.

What strange advice this would seem to many, to cast their bread upon the waters, which would seem to them like throwing it away! What more direct method to lose our bread than to go and throw it into the sea? But the wise man tells us, No, it is not lost; you will find it again after many days. It is not sunk, but you commit it to Providence; you commit it to the winds and waves; however it will come about to you, and you will find it again after many days. Even

101

if you have to wait many days, you will find it at last, at a time when you most need it. Whoever gives to the poor lends to the Lord, and God is not one of those who will not pay back what is lent to him. If you lend anything to God, you commit it into faithful hands. 'He hath that pity on the poor lendeth to the Lord, and that which he hath given will he pay him again' (Proverbs 19:17). God will not only pay you back, but he will pay you with a lot of interest: 'Give, and it shall be given you', that is, in 'good measure, pressed down, and shaken together, and running over' (Luke 6:38).

Men do not regard as lost what is lent at interest; but what is given in charity is lent to the Lord, and he repays with a lot of interest. 'The liberal deviseth liberal things, and by liberal things shall he stand' (Isaiah 32:8). Here I would particularly observe:

Eternal riches will be your reward: If you give with a spirit of true charity, you will be rewarded in what is infinitely more valuable than what you give – eternal riches in heaven. 'Whosoever shall give to drink unto one of these little ones, a cup of cold water only, in the name of a disciple; verily I say unto you, he shall in no wise lose his reward' (Matthew 10:42).

Giving to our needy brothers is in Scripture called laying up treasure in heaven, in bags that do not grow old. 'Sell that ye have, and give alms; provide yourselves bags which wax not old, a treasure in the heavens that faileth not, where no thief approacheth, neither moth corrupteth' (Luke 12:33). Men, when they have laid up their money in their chests, do not suppose that they have thrown it away but, on the contrary, that it is laid up safe. Much less is treasure thrown away when it is laid up in heaven. What is laid up there is much safer than what is laid up in chests or cabinets.

You cannot lay up treasure on earth without it being liable to be stolen, or otherwise to fail. But there no thief approaches, nor does moth corrupt. It is committed to God's care, and he will keep it safely for you; and when you die, you will receive it with infinite interest. Instead of a part of your earthly substance thus given, you will receive heavenly riches, on which you may live in the greatest fullness, honour, and happiness, to all eternity; and will never need anything. After feeding with some of your bread those who cannot recompense you, you will be rewarded at the resurrection, and eat bread in the kingdom of God. 'When thou makest a feast, call the poor, the maimed, the lame, and the blind: and thou shalt be blessed; for they cannot recompense thee: for thou shalt be recompensed at the resurrection of the just. And when one of them that sat at meat with him, heard these things, he said unto him, Blessed is he that shall eat meat in the kingdom of God' (Luke 14:13–16).

Giving for moral reasons and giving through grace: If you give to the needy just in the exercise of moral virtue, you will be in the way to gain greatly by it in your temporal interest. Those who give in the exercise of a *gracious* charity are in the way to be gainers both here and hereafter; and those who give in the exercise of a *moral* bounty and liberality have many temporal promises made to them. We learn by the word of God that they are in the way to be prospered in their outward affairs. Ordinarily such people do not lose by it, but such a blessing attends their concerns that they are paid doubly for it: 'There is that scattereth, and yet increaseth; there is that withholdeth more than is meet, but it tendeth to poverty. The liberal soul shall be made fat: and he that watereth, shall be watered also himself' (Proverbs 11:24–25). 'He that giveth to the poor, shall not lack' (Proverbs 28:27).

Giving to the poor is like sowing seed: When men give to the needy, they sow seed for a crop, as it were. When men sow their seed, they seem to throw it away; yet they do not look upon it as thrown away, because, though they do not expect the same back, they expect much more as the fruit of it; and if it is not certain that they will have a crop, they are still willing to run the risk, for that is the ordinary way men obtain increase. So it is when people give to the poor; though the promises of gaining thereby, in our outward circumstances, perhaps are not absolute, yet it is as much the ordinary consequence of it as increase is of sowing seed. Giving to the poor is in this respect compared to sowing seed: 'In the morning sow thy seed, and in the evening withhold not thine hand: for thou knowest not whether shall prosper, either this or that, or whether they both shall be alike good' (Ecclesiastes 11:6). By withholding the hand, the wise man means, not giving to the poor. (See verses 1–2.) It intimates that giving to the poor is as likely a way to obtain prosperity and increase as sowing seed in a field.

The farmer does not look on his seed as lost, but is glad that he has opportunity to sow it. It does not grieve him that he has land to be sown, but he rejoices in it. For the same reason we should not be grieved that we find needy people to bestow our charity on; for this is as much an opportunity to obtain increase as the other.

Some people may think this is strange doctrine; and it is to be feared that not many will so far believe it as to give to the poor with as much cheerfulness as they sow their ground. However, it is the very doctrine of the word of God: 'But this I say, He which soweth sparingly, shall reap also sparingly: and he which soweth bountifully, shall reap also bountifully. Every man according as he purposeth in his heart, so let him give; not grudgingly, or of necessity: for God loveth a cheerful giver. And God is able to make all grace abound towards you; that ye always having all sufficiency in all things, may abound to every good work' (2 Corinthians 9:6–8).

It is easy for God to make up to men what they give in charity: Many give very little consideration to how their prosperity or failure in their outward affairs depends upon Providence. There are a thousand turns of Providence, to which their affairs are liable, by which God may either add to their outward substance or diminish it a great deal more than they are ordinarily called to give to their neighbours. How easy is it with God to diminish what they possess by sickness in their families, by drought, or frost, or mildew, or vermin; by unfortunate accidents, by entanglements in their affairs, or disappointments in their business! And how easy is it with God to increase their substance, by suitable seasons, or by health and strength; by giving them fair opportunities for promoting their interest in their dealings with men; by conducting them in his providence so that they attain their ambitions; and by innumerable other ways which might be mentioned! How often it is that only one act of providence in a man's affairs either adds to his estate, or diminishes it, more than he would need to give to the poor in a whole year.

This is the way to receive God's blessing: God has told us that this is the way to have his blessing attending our affairs. Thus, in the text: 'Thou shalt surely give him, and thine heart shall not be grieved when thou givest unto him; because that for this thing the Lord thy God shall bless thee in all thy works, and in all that thou puttest thine hand unto' (verse 10). 'He that hath a bountiful eye, shall be blessed' (Proverbs 22:9). It is a remarkable evidence how little many men realize the things of religion, whatever they claim; how little they realize that the Scripture is the word of God, or if it is, that he speaks true; that not withstanding all the promises made in the Scripture to bounty to the poor, yet they are so reluctant to perform this duty, and are so afraid to trust God with a little of their estates. Observation may confirm the same thing which the word of God teaches on this subject. God, in his providence, generally smiles upon and prospers those men who are of a liberal, charitable, bountiful spirit.

God has threatened to curse the uncharitable: God has threatened to follow with his curse those who are uncharitable to the poor: 'He that giveth to the poor shall not lack; but he that hideth his eyes, shall have many a curse' (Proverbs 28:27). It says *he that hideth his eyes* because this is the way of uncharitable men; they hide their eyes from seeing the needs of their neighbour. A charitable person, whose heart disposes him to bounty and liberality, will be quick-sighted to discern the needs of others. They will not have any difficulty in finding out who is in need; they will see objects enough of their charity, wherever they go.

On the other hand, anyone who is of a niggardly spirit, so that it goes against the grain to give anything, will always be at a loss for objects of charity. Such men excuse themselves by saying that they do not find anyone to give to. They hide their eyes, and do not want to see their neighbour's needs. If a particular object is presented, they will not very readily see his circumstances; they are a long while being convinced that he is an object of charity. They hide their eyes; and it is not an easy thing to make them aware of the necessities and distresses of their neighbour, or at least to convince them that his necessities are such that they ought to give him anything much.

Other men, who are of a bountiful spirit, can very easily see the objects of charity; but the uncharitable are very unapt both to see the proper objects of charity and to see their obligations to perform this duty. The reason is that they are of the sort spoken of here by the wise man: *they hide their eyes*. Men will readily see where they are *willing* to see; but where they hate to see, they will hide their eyes.

God says, the person who hides his eyes in this case will have many a curse. Such a person is on the way to being cursed in soul and body, in both his spiritual and temporal affairs. We have already shown how those who are charitable to the poor are on the way to being blessed. There are so many promises of the divine blessing that we may look upon it as being just as much the way to be blessed in our outward concerns as sowing seed in a field is the way to receive increase. And being close and uncharitable is as much the way to be followed with a curse as being charitable is the way to be followed with a blessing. To withhold more than is right tends as much to poverty and scattering tends to increase (Proverbs 11:24). Therefore, if you withhold more than is right, you will cross your own disposition, and will frustrate your own end. What you seek by withholding from your neighbour is your own temporal interest and outward state; but if you believe the Scriptures to be the word of God, you must believe that you cannot take a more direct course to lose, to be crossed and cursed in your temporal interest, than this of withholding from your indigent neighbour.

You may yourself be in need: Consider that you do not know what calamitous and necessitous circumstances you yourselves or your children may be in. Perhaps you are ready to bless yourselves in your hearts as though there were no danger of your being brought into calamitous and distressing circumstances. There is at present no prospect of it; and you hope you will be able to provide well for your children. But you little consider what a shifting, changing, uncertain world you live in, and how often it has happened that people have been reduced from the greatest prosperity to the greatest adversity, and how often the children of the rich have been reduced to pinching want.

You do not know what calamitous circumstances you may be in yourself in this changeable, uncertain world. You do not know what circumstances you or your children may be brought into by captivity, or other unthought-of providences. Providence governs all things. Perhaps you may trust to your own wisdom to continue your prosperity; but you cannot alter what God determines and orders in providence, as in the words immediately following the text quoted above: 'If the clouds be full of rain, they empty themselves upon the earth; and if the tree fall toward the south or toward the north; in the place where the tree falleth, there it shall be' (Ecclesiastes 11:3–4) – i.e. you cannot alter the determinations of Providence. You may trust to your own wisdom for future prosperity; but if God has ordained adversity, it *shall come*: as the clouds when full of rain empty themselves upon the earth, so what is in the womb of Providence will surely come to pass. And as Providence casts the tree, whether towards the south or towards the north, whether for prosperity or adversity, there it shall be, for all that you can do to alter it – as the wise man says, 'Consider the work of God; for who can make that straight which he hath made crooked?' (Ecclesiastes 7:13).

This consideration, that you do not know what calamity and necessity you or your children may be in yourselves, tends very powerfully to enforce this duty in several ways.

1. It may make you consider how your hearts would be affected if it

should be so. If it should happen that you or some of your children should be brought into such circumstances as those of your neighbours, how grievous it would be to you! Now perhaps you say of this or that poor neighbour that they can do well enough; if they are pinched a little, they can live. Thus you can make light of their difficulties. But if Providence should so order it that you or your children should be brought into the same circumstances, would you make light of them then? Would you not use another sort of language about it? Would you not think that your case was such as needed the kindness of your neighbours? Would you not think that they ought to be ready to help you? And would you not take it hard if you saw a contrary spirit in them, and saw that they made light of your difficulties?

If one of your children should be brought to poverty by captivity or otherwise, how would your hearts be affected in such a case? If you should hear that some people had taken pity on your child and had been very bountiful to it, would you not think that they did well? Would you be at all apt to accuse them of folly or profuseness in giving so much to it?

2. If ever there should be such a time, your kindness to others now will be just a laying up against such a time. If you yourselves should be brought into calamity and necessity, then you would find what you have given in charity to others lying ready in store for you. The person who gives to the poor will not lack.

Giving to the needy is like laying up against winter, or against a time of calamity. It is the best way of laying up for yourselves and for your children. Children in a time of need very often find their fathers' bread, that bread which their fathers had cast upon the waters. 'I have been young and now am old, yet have I not seen the righteous forsaken, nor his seed begging bread' (Psalm 37:25). Why? What is the reason of it? It follows in the next verse: 'He is ever merciful and lendeth, and his seed is blessed.'

Whether the time will ever come or not, that we or our children are in distressing need of bread, doubtless evil will be on the earth. We will have our times of calamity, in which we will stand in great need of God's pity and help, if not of that of our fellow-creatures.

And God has promised that at such a time anyone who has been charitable in spirit and practice will find help: 'Blessed is he that considereth the poor; the Lord will deliver him in time of trouble. The Lord will prepare him, and keep him alive, and he shall be blessed upon the earth; and thou wilt not deliver him until the will of his enemies. The Lord will strengthen him upon the bed of languishing: thou wilt make all his bed in his sickness' (Psalm 44:1–4). Those who have been merciful and liberal to others in their distress God will not forget, but will so order it that they will have help when they are in distress. Indeed, their children will reap the fruit of it in the day of trouble.

3. God has threatened uncharitable people that if ever they come to be in calamity and distress they will be left helpless: 'Whoso stoppeth his ears at the cry of the poor, he shall cry himself and not be heard' (Proverbs 21:3).

Objections which are sometimes made to the exercise of charity

I proceed now to answer some objections which are sometimes made against this duty.

A wrong spirit?

'I am a natural state, and if I gave the poor, I would not do it with a right spirit, and so would get nothing from it.' To this I answer:

This is the way to prosper

We have shown already that a temporal blessing is promised to a moral bounty and liberality. This is the way to be prospered; this is the way to increase. We find in Scripture many promises of temporal blessings to moral virtues, such as diligence in our business, justice in our dealings, faithfulness, temperance. In the same way, there are many blessings promised to bounty and liberality.

The same applies to other duties

You may as well make the same objection against any other duty of religion. You may as well object against keeping the sabbath, against prayer, or public worship, or against doing anything at all in religion; for while you are in a natural state, you do not do any of these duties with a right spirit. If you say you do these duties because God has commanded or required them of you, and you will sin greatly if you neglect them – that you will increase your guilt, and so expose yourselves to the greater damnation and punishment – the same may be said of the neglect of this duty; neglecting it is as provoking to God.

If you say that you read, and pray, and attend public worship, because that is the appointed way for you to seek salvation, so is bounty to the poor, as much as those. The appointed way for us to seek the favour of God and eternal life is to perform all known duties, of which giving to the poor is one as well known and as necessary as reading the Scriptures, praying, or any other. Showing mercy to the poor belongs as much to the appointed way of seeking salvation as any other duty whatever. Therefore this is the way in which Daniel directed Nebuchadnezzar to seek mercy: 'Wherefore, O king, let my counsel be acceptable to thee, and break off thy sins by righteousness, and thine iniquities by *showing mercy to the poor*' (Daniel 4:27).

More harm than good?

'If I am liberal and bountiful, I shall only make a righteousness of it, and so it will do me more harm than good.' To this I say:

The same applies to other duties

The same answer may be made to this as to the previous objection, namely, that you may as well make the same objection against doing any religious or moral duty at all. If this is a sufficient objection against the deeds of charity, then it is a sufficient objection to prayer; for nothing is more common than for people to make a righteousness of their prayers. Similarly, it is a good objection against your keeping the sabbath, or attending any public worship, or ever reading the Bible; for you are in danger of making a righteousness of all these things. Indeed, if the objection is good against deeds of charity, then it is as good against acts of justice; and you may neglect to speak the truth, may neglect to pay your debts, may neglect acts of common humanity; for of all those things you are in danger of making a righteousness. So if your objection is good, you may throw up all religion, and live like heathens or atheists, and may be thieves, robbers, fornicators, adulterers, murderers, and commit all the sins that you can think of, lest if you should do otherwise, you should make a righteousness of your conduct.

God makes no exception

Your objection implies that it is not best for you to do as God commands and counsels you to do. We find many commands in Scripture to be charitable to the poor; the Bible is full of them; and you are not excepted from those commands. God makes no exception of any particular kinds of persons that are especially in danger of making a righteousness of what they do; and God often directs and counsels persons to this duty. Now will you presume to say that God has not directed you to the best way? He has advised you to do this; but you think it not best for you, but that it would do you more harm than good if you did it. You think there is other counsel better than God's, and that it is the best way for you to go contrary to God's commands.

You have not benefited?

'I have in times past given to the poor, but never found myself the better for it. I have heard ministers preach that giving to the poor was the way to prosper, but I do not perceive that I am more prosperous than I was before. Indeed, I have met with many misfortunes, crosses, and disappointments in my affairs since.' And it may be that some will say, 'That very year, or soon after the very time, I had been giving to the poor, hoping to be blessed for it, I met with great losses, and things were hard for me; and therefore I do not find that what I hear preached about giving to the poor being the way to be blessed and prosperous is true in my experience.'

To this objection I shall answer several things:

The promises are not to the grudging giver

Perhaps you looked for the fulfilment of the promises too soon, before you had fulfilled the condition. In particular, perhaps you have been so sparing and grudging in your kindness to the poor that what you have done has been rather the sign of a covetous, niggardly spirit than of any bounty or liberality. The promises are not made to everyone who gives anything at all to the poor, however little, and in whatever way it is given. You mistook the promise if you understood them to mean this. A man may give something to the poor and yet be entitled to no promise, either temporal or spiritual. The promises are made to *mercy* and *liberality*. But a man may give something, and yet be so niggardly and grudging in it that what he gives may be, as the apostle calls it, a matter of covetousness. What he does may be more a sign of his covetousness and closeness than anything else. But there are no promises made to men's expressing their covetousness.

Perhaps what you gave was not freely given, but as it were of necessity. It was grudging; your hearts were grieved when they gave. And if you gave considerably once or twice, that does not answer the rule. It may be, for all that, that in the general course of your lives you have been far from being kind and liberal to your neighbours. Perhaps you thought that because you gave a few shillings to the poor once or twice, you were entitled to the promises of being blessed in all your concerns, and of increasing and being established by liberal things; though in general you have lived in a faulty neglect of the duty of charity. You raise objections from experience, before you have made trial. To give once, or twice, or three times, is not to make trial, even if you give considerably. You cannot make any trial unless you become a liberal person, or

unless you become such that you may truly be said to practise liberality and bounty. Let one who truly does this, and has been like this
in the general course of his life, tell what he has found by experience.

You do not know how much worse things might have been

If you have been liberal to the poor, and have met with calamities
since, how can you tell how much greater calamities and losses you
might have met with if you had been otherwise? You say you have
met with crosses, and disappointments, and frowns. If you
expected to meet with no trouble in the world, because you gave to
the poor, you mistook the matter. Though many great promises are
made to the liberal, God has nowhere promised that they will not
find this world a world of trouble. It will be so to all. Man is born to
sorrow, and must expect no other than to meet with sorrow here.
But how can you tell how much greater sorrow you would have met
with if you had been close and unmerciful to the poor? How can
you tell how much greater losses you would have met with? Have
none ever met with greater frowns in their outward affairs than you
have?

God may have further blessing in store for you

How can you tell what blessings God still has in reserve for you if
you do but continue in well-doing? Although God has promised
great blessings to liberality to the poor, he has still not limited
himself as to when he will bestow them. If you have not yet seen any
evident fruit of your kindness to the poor, the time may yet come
when you will see it remarkably, and that at a time when you most
stand in need of it. You cast your bread upon the waters, and looked
for it, and expected to find it again straightaway. And sometimes it
is so; but this is not promised: it is promised that 'thou shalt find it
again *after many days*'. God knows how to choose a time for you
better than you do yourselves. You should therefore wait for his
time. If you go on in well-doing, God may bring it to you when you
stand most in need.

It may be that there is some winter coming, some day of trouble; and God keeps your bread for you against that time; and then God will give you good measure, and pressed down, and shaken together, and running over. We must trust in God's word to give the promised reward whether we can see how it is done or not. The words of the wise man in Ecclesiastes 11:4 are relevant: 'He that observeth the winds shall not sow; and he that regardeth the clouds shall not reap.' In this context the wise man is speaking of charity to the poor, and comparing it to sowing seed; and advises us to trust Providence for success in that, as we do in sowing seed. Someone who looks at the winds and clouds to forecast the right time to sow, and will not trust Providence with it, is not likely to sow, nor to have bread-corn. So anyone who will not trust Providence for the reward of his charity to the poor is likely to go without the blessing. After the words just quoted follows this advice: 'In the morning sow thy seed, and in the evening withhold not thine hand; for thou knowest not whether shall prosper, either this or that, or whether they both shall be alike good' (verse 6). Therefore 'let us not be weary in well doing; for in due season we shall reap, if we faint not' (Galatians 6:9). You think you have not reaped yet. Whether you have or not, go on still in giving and doing good; and if you do so, you will reap in due time. God only knows the due time, the best time, for you to reap.

Charity just to those in extremity?

Some may object against charity to such or such particular persons that they are not obliged to give them anything, for though they are needy, they are not in extremity. It is true they meet with difficulty, yet not so much that they cannot live, though they suffer some hardships.

But it does not answer the rules of Christian charity to relieve only those who are reduced to extremity, as might be abundantly shown. I shall here mention just two things as evidences of it.

We are to treat one another as brothers

We are commanded to love and treat one another as brothers: 'Have compassion one of another; love as brethren; be pitiful' (1 Peter 3:8). Now, do brothers refuse to help one another, and to do anything for each other's comfort, and for the relief of each other's difficulties, only when they are in extremity? Does it not become brothers and sisters to have a more friendly disposition towards one another than this comes to, and to be ready to have compassion on one another under difficulties, even if they are not extreme?

The rule of the gospel is that when we see our brother under any difficulty or burden, we should be ready to bear the burden with him: 'Bear ye one another's burdens, and so fulfil the law of Christ' (Galatians 6:2). Similarly, we are commanded 'by love to serve one another' (Galatians 5:13). The Christian spirit will make us apt to sympathize with our neighbour when we see him in any difficulty: 'Rejoice with them that do rejoice, and weep with them that weep' (Romans 12:15). When our neighbour is in difficulty, he is afflicted; and we ought to have such a spirit of love to him as to be afflicted with him in his affliction. And if we ought to be afflicted with him, then it will follow that we ought to be ready to relieve him, because, if we are afflicted with him, in relieving him we relieve ourselves. His relief is our own relief, in so far as his affliction is our affliction. Christianity teaches us to be afflicted in our neighbour's affliction; and nature teaches us to relieve ourselves when afflicted.

We should behave towards one another like brothers that are fellow travellers; for we are pilgrims and strangers here on earth and are on a journey. Now, if brothers are on a journey together, and one meets with difficulty on the way, does it not become the rest to help him, not only in the extremity of broken bones, or the like, but as to provision for the journey if his own fall short? It becomes his fellow travellers to afford him a supply out of their stores, and not to be over-exact, and fearful lest they give him too much: for it is only provision for a journey; and all are supplied when they get to their journey's end.

We are to love our neighbour as ourselves

That we should relieve our neighbour only when in extremity does not agree with the rule of loving our neighbour as ourselves. That rule implies that our love towards our neighbour should work in the same manner, and express itself in the same ways, as our love towards ourselves. We are very conscious of our own difficulties; we should also be readily conscious of theirs. Out of love to ourselves, when we are in difficulties and suffer hardships, we are concerned for our relief, and we seek relief and put ourselves out for it. And as we would love our neighbour as ourselves, we ought in the same way to be concerned when our neighbour is in difficulty, and to seek his relief. We are much concerned about our own difficulties, even if we are not reduced to extremity, and are willing in those cases to put ourselves out for our own relief. Similarly, if we want to love our neighbour as ourselves, we should in the same way put ourselves out to obtain relief for him, even if his difficulties are not extreme.

The undeserving

Some may object against charity to a particular person because he is a bad sort of person; he does not deserve people to be kind to him; he is very bad-tempered and ungrateful, and particularly because he has not deserved well of them, but has ill-treated them, has been harmful to them, and even now entertains an ill spirit against them.

But we are obliged to relieve people in need, notwithstanding these things, both by the general and particular rules of God's word.

The general rules of Scripture

We are obliged to do so by the general rules of Scripture. I shall mention two.

We are to love our neighbour as ourselves: A man may be our *neighbour* even if he is a bad sort of man, and even our enemy, as Christ himself teaches us in his discourse with the lawyers (Luke 10:25ff.). A certain lawyer came to Christ and asked him what he should do to inherit eternal life. Christ asked him what was written in the law. He answers, 'Thou shalt love the Lord thy God with all thy heart, and with all thy soul, and with all thy strength, and with all thy mind; and thy neighbour as thyself.' Christ tells him that if he does this, he will live. But then the lawyer asks him who his neighbour is, because it was a received doctrine among the Pharisees that no man was their neighbour except their friends, and those of the same people and religion. Christ answered him by a parable, or story, of a certain man who went down from Jerusalem to Jericho, and fell among thieves, who stripped him of his raiment, and wounded him, and departed from him, leaving him half-dead. Soon after, there came that way a priest, who saw the poor man that had been thus cruelly treated by the thieves; but he passed by without helping him. The same was done by a Levite. But a certain Samaritan coming that way, as soon as he saw the half-dead man, had compassion on him, took him up, bound up his wounds, set him on his own beast, carried him to the inn, and took care of him, paying the innkeeper money for his past and future expense; and promising him still more, if he should find it necessary to be at more expense on behalf of the man.

Then Christ asks the lawyer which of these three – the priest, the Levite, or the Samaritan – was neighbour to the man that fell along thieves. Christ proposed this in such a manner that the lawyer could not help admitting that the Samaritan did well in relieving the Jew, that he did the duty of a neighbour to him. Now, there was an inveterate enmity between the Jews and the Samaritans. They hated one another more than any other nation in the world and the Samaritans were exceedingly troublesome to the Jews; yet we see that Christ teaches that the Jews ought to play the part of neighbours to the Samaritans; i.e. to love them as themselves; for it was that of which Christ was speaking.

And the consequence was plain. If the Samaritan was neighbour to the distressed Jew, then the Jews, by the same reasoning were neighbours to the Samaritans. If the Samaritan did well in relieving a Jew that was his enemy, than the Jews would do well in relieving the Samaritans, their enemies.

What I particularly observe is that Christ here plainly teaches that our enemies, those that abuse and injure us, are our neighbours, and therefore come under the rule of loving our neighbour as ourselves.

We are to love one another as Christ has loved us: 'A new commandment I give unto you, that ye love one another; as I have loved you, that ye also love one another' (John 13:34). Christ calls it a *new* commandment, with respect to that old commandment of loving our neighbour as ourselves. This command of loving our neighbour as Christ has loved us opens our duty to us in a new manner, and in a further degree than that did. We must not only love our neighbour as ourselves, but as Christ has loved us. We have the same again in John 15:12: 'This is my commandment, that ye love one another, as I have loved you.'

Now, the meaning of this is not that we should love one another to the same *degree* that Christ loved us (though there ought to be a proportion, considering our nature and capacity); but that we should exercise our love to one another in a similar *manner*. As, for instance, Christ has loved us so as to be willing to deny himself, and to differ greatly in order to help us; so should we be willing to deny ourselves in order to help one another. Christ loved us, and showed us great kindness though we were far below him; similarly, we should show kindness to those of our fellow men who are far below us. Christ denied himself to help us, though we are not able to recompense him; similarly, we should be willing to put ourselves out to help our neighbour, freely expecting nothing back. Christ loved us, was kind to us, and was willing to relieve us though we were very evil and hateful, of an evil disposition, not deserving any good, but deserving only to be hated, and treated with indignation; similarly, we should be willing to be kind to those who are of a bad disposition, and are very undeserving. Christ loved us, and put himself out to relieve us, though we were his enemies, and had ill-treated him; similarly we, if we want to love one another as Christ has loved us, should relieve those who are our enemies, hate us, have an ill spirit towards us, and have ill-treated us.

Particular rules

We are obliged to this duty by many particular rules. We are particularly required to be kind to the unthankful and to the evil; and therein to follow the example of our heavenly Father, who causes his sun to rise on the evil and on the good, and sends rain on the just and on the unjust. We are obliged not only to be kind to those who are so to us, but to those that hate us and treat us with spite. I need not mention the particular passages which speak to this effect.

Not but that when people are virtuous and pious, and have a grateful disposition, and are friendly disposed towards us, they are more the objects of our charity for it, and our obligation to kindness to them is the greater. Yet if things are otherwise, that does not make them unfit objects of our charity, not set us free from obligation to kindness towards them.

Nothing to spare?

Some may object from their own circumstances that they have nothing to spare; they have not got more than enough for themselves. I answer:

In some cases we are not obliged to give

It must doubtless be admitted that in some cases people, because of their own circumstances, are not obliged to give to others. For instance, if there is a collection for the poor, they are not obliged to join in the collection if they are in as much need as those for whom the collection is made. It savours of ridiculous vanity in them to contribute with others for those who are no more needy than they. It savours of a proud desire to conceal their own circumstances, and an affectation of having them thought better than they are in fact.

No one thinks he has more than enough

There are scarcely any who may not make this objection, as they interpret it. There is no person who may not say he has not more than enough for himself, as he may mean by *enough*. He may mean that he has not got more than he desires, or more than he can dispose of to his own advantage; or not so much but that, if he had anything less, he would look upon himself in worse circumstances than he is now. He will admit that he could live if he had less; but then he will say he could not live so well. Rich men may say that they have not more than enough for themselves, as they may mean by it. They need it all, they may say, to support their honour and dignity, as is proper for the situation in which they stand. Those who are poor, to be sure, will say *they* have not too much for themselves; those who are of the middle sort will say *they* have not too much for themselves; and the rich will say *they* have not too much for themselves. Thus no one will be found to give to the poor.

We should be willing to suffer

In many cases, by the rules of the gospel, we may be obliged to give to others when we cannot do it without suffering ourselves. For example, if our neighbours difficulties and necessities are much greater than our own, and we see that he is not likely to be relieved otherwise, we should be willing to suffer with him, and to take part of his burden on ourselves; otherwise how is that rule of *bearing one another's burdens* fulfilled? If we are never obliged to relieve other people's burdens except when we can do it without burdening ourselves, then how do we bear our neighbour's burdens, when we bear no burden at all? We may not have a surplus, yet we may be obliged to give relief to others who are in much greater need – as appears from the rule in Luke 3:11, 'He that hath two coats, let him impart to him that hath none; and he that hath meat, let him do likewise.' Indeed, those who are very poor may be obliged to give for the relief of others in much greater distress than they. If there is no other way of relief, those who have the lightest burden are still obliged to take some part of their neighbour's burden, to make it the more supportable. A brother may be obliged to help a brother in extremity, though they are both very much in need. The apostle commends the Macedonian Christians for being liberal to their brothers, though they themselves were in deep poverty: 'Moreover, brethren, we do you to wit of the grace of God bestowed in the churches of Macedonia: how in a great trial of affliction, the abundance of their joy, and their deep poverty, abounded unto the riches of their liberality' (2 Corinthians 8:1–2).

We should spare seed for sowing

Those who do not have too much for themselves are willing to spare seed to sow, that they may have fruit later on. Perhaps they need what they scatter in the field, and seem to throw away. They may need it for bread for their families; yet they will spare seed to sow, that they may provide for the future, and may have increase. But we have already shown that giving to the poor is compared in Scripture to sowing seed, and is as much the way to increase as the sowing of seed is. It does not tend to poverty, but the contrary; it is not the way to diminish our substance, but to increase it. The only difficulty in this matter is in trusting God with what we give, in trusting his promises. If men could only trust the faithfulness of God to his own promises, they would give freely.

Uncertain whether a person is an object of charity?

Some people may object concerning a particular person that they do not certainly know whether he is an object of charity or not. They are not perfectly acquainted with his circumstances; neither do they know what sort of man he is. They do not know whether he is in need as he claims. Or if they know this, they do not know how he came to be in need; whether it were not by his own idleness or prodigality. Thus they argue that they cannot be obliged till they know these things for certain. I reply:

Nabal is condemned for this

This is Nabal's objection, for which he is greatly condemned in Scripture (see 1 Samuel 25). David in his exiled state came and begged relief of Nabal. Nabal objected: 'Who is David? And who is the son of Jesse? There be many servants nowadays that break away every man from his master. Shall I then take my bread and my water, and my flesh that I have killed for my shearers, and give it unto men, whom I know not whence they be?' (verse 10–11). His objection was that David was a stranger to him; he did not know who he was, nor what his circumstances were. He did not know that he was not a runaway; and he was not obliged to support and harbour a runaway. He objected that he did not know that he was a proper object of charity; that he did not know that he was not very much the contrary.

But Abigail did not countenance his behaviour in this respect at all, but greatly condemned it. She calls him a man of Belial, and says that he was like his name – Nabal was his name, and folly was with him. And her behaviour was very contrary to his; and she is greatly condemned for it. The Holy Spirit tells us that 'she was a woman of good understanding' (verse 3). At the same time God exceedingly frowned on Nabal's behaviour on this occasion, as we are informed that about ten days afterwards God 'smote Nabal, that he died' (verse 38).

This story is doubtless told us partly so that we should not be too scrupulous about the object of our charity, and making it merely an objection against charity to others that we do not know their circumstances for certain. It is true, when we have opportunity to become properly acquainted with their circumstances it is well to embrace it, and to be influenced in some measure by probability in such cases is not to be condemned. Yet it is better to give to several that are not objects of charity than to send away empty one that is.

We have to be kind to strangers

We are commanded to be kind to strangers when we do not know them or their circumstances. This is commanded in many places, but I will mention only one: 'Be not forgetful to entertain strangers; for thereby some have entertained angels unawares' (Hebrews 12:2). By strangers here the apostle means someone we do not know, and whose circumstances we do not know; as is evident from the word 'for thereby some have entertained angels unawares'. Those who entertained angels unawares did not know the people they entertained, nor their circumstances – otherwise, how could it be unawares?

Not giving to the poor till they ask

Some may say they are not obliged to give to the poor till they ask. 'If anyone is in need, let him come and make his straits known to me, and then it will be time enough for me to give to him. Or if he needs a public appeal, let him come and ask. I do not know that the congregation or church is obliged to relieve till they ask relief.' I answer:

Do the greatest kindness

It is surely most charitable to relieve the needy in whatever way will do them the greatest kindness. Now it is certain that we shall do them a greater kindness by inquiring into their circumstances and relieving them, without forcing them to beg. None of us, if it were our own case, would not look upon it as more kind of our neighbours to inquire into our circumstances and help us of their own accord. To force our neighbours to beg in order to obtain relief is painful. It is more charitable, more brotherly, more becoming Christians and the disciples of Jesus, to do it without. I think this is self-evident, and needs no proof.

The nature of the liberal person

It does not agree with the character of the liberal man given in Scripture, namely, one that devises liberal things (Isaiah 32:8). It is not to devise liberal things if we neglect all liberality till the poor come begging to us. But to inquire who stand in need of our charity and to contrive to relieve them in the way that will do them the greatest kindness – that is to devise liberal things.

We would not commend a man for doing so to his own brother

If a man had an own brother or sister in great straits and he were well able to supply them, claiming that if he or she wanted anything they should come and ask for it, we would hardly think such a person behaved like a brother. Christians are commanded to look upon one another as brothers in Christ, and to treat one another as such.

We should commend the opposite action

We should commend others for taking a method contrary to that which is proposed to the objector. If we should hear or read of a people who were so charitable, who took such care of the poor, and were so concerned that none among them should suffer if they were proper objects of charity; that they would diligently inquire into the circumstances of their neighbours to find out who were needy, and liberally supply them of their own accord; I say, if we should hear or read of such a people, would it not seem good to us? Would we not think better of that people, on that account?

'It is their own fault'

'He has brought himself into this state by his own fault'. In reply, it must be considered what you mean by his fault.

We should share our gifts

If you mean a lack of the natural ability to manage affairs to advantage, that is to be considered as his calamity. Such an ability is a gift that God bestows on some, and not on others; and it is not owing to themselves. You ought to be thankful that God has given you such a gift, which he has denied to the person in question. And it will be a very suitable way for you to show your thankfulness, to help those to whom that gift is denied, and let them share the benefit of it with you. This is as reasonable as that anyone to whom Providence has given sight should be willing to help someone to whom sight is denied, and that someone who has no sight of his own should have the benefit of the sight of others; or, as that someone to whom God has given wisdom should be willing that the ignorant should have the benefit of his knowledge.

'They did not think'

If they have been reduced to want by some oversight, and are to be blamed that they did not think for themselves, that does still not free us from all obligation to charity towards them. If we always refused to help people because of that, we would be making their failure to think, and their imprudent act, an unpardonable crime, quite contrary to the rules of the gospel, which insists so much upon forgiveness. We would not be disposed to resent such an oversight so highly in anyone for whom we have a dear affection, such as our children, or our friends. We would not refuse to help them in that necessity and distress which they brought upon themselves by their own unthinking behaviour. But we ought to have a dear affection and concern for the welfare of all our fellow Christians, whom we should love as brothers, and as Christ has loved us.

We must forgive idleness and prodigality

If they have come to be in need by the vice of idleness and prodigality, we are still not excused from all obligation to relieve them, unless they continue in those vices. If they do not continue in those vices, the rules of the gospel direct us to forgive them; and if their fault is forgiven, it will not remain to be a bar in the way of our charitably relieving them. If we do otherwise, we shall act in a manner very contrary to the rule of *loving one another as Christ has loved us*. Now Christ has loved us, pitied us, and greatly put himself out to relieve us from that want and misery which we brought on ourselves by our own folly and wickedness. We foolishly and perversely threw away those riches with which we were provided, upon which we might have lived and been happy to all eternity.

We must be charitable to their families

If they still continue in the same courses, that does still not excuse us from charity to their families that are innocent. If we cannot relieve those of their families without their having something of it, that still ought not to be a bar in the way of our charity; and that because it is supposed that those of their families are proper objects of charity; and those that are so, we are bound to relieve: the command is positive and absolute. If we look upon that which the heads of the families have of what we give as entirely lost, we had still better lost something of our estate than allow those who are really proper objects of charity to remain without relief.

'Others do not do their duty'

Some may object and say, 'Others do not do their duty. If others did their duty, the poor would be sufficiently supplied. If others did as much as we in proportion to their ability and obligation, the poor would have enough to help them out of their straits.' Or some may say, 'It is other people's business more than it is ours. They have relations who ought to help them; or there are others whose business it is rather than ours.'

My answer is that we ought to relieve those who are in need, even if they are brought to it through others' fault. If our neighbour is poor, even though other people are to blame that it is so, that does not excuse us from helping him. If it is other people's business more than ours, still if those others neglect their duty and our neighbour therefore remains in need, we may be obliged to relieve him. If someone is brought into straits through the injustice of others, such as by thieves or robbers, as the poor Jew whom the Samaritan relieved, we may still be obliged to relieve him, even though it is not our fault that he is in need, but that of other people. And whether that fault is through commission or neglect does not alter the case.

As to the poor Jew that fell among thieves between Jerusalem and Jericho, it was the thieves who brought him into that distress who were responsible, rather than anyone else. Yet seeing they would not do it, others were not excused; and the Samaritan did no more than his duty, relieving him as he did, though it was really other people's responsibility.

Thus a man may have children or other relations who are responsible for relieving him, but if they will not do it, the obligation to relieve him falls upon others. So for the same reason we should do all the more for the relief of the poor, because others neglect to do their part, or what is their responsibility; and that is because by the neglect of others to do their part they need the more, their need is the greater.

'It is the government's responsibility'

The law makes provision for the poor, and obliges the respective towns in which they live to provide for them; therefore some people argue that there is no occasion for individual persons to exercise any charity in this way. They say the case is not the same with us now as it was in the early church; for then Christians were under a heathen government, and however much the charity of Christians in those times is to be commended, there is no need for private charity now because of our different circumstances. In the state in which Christians are now, provision is made for the poor in other ways.

This objection is built upon the two suppositions, both which I suppose are false:

The law only relieves those in the worst need

It is based on the idea that the towns are obliged by law to relieve everyone who otherwise would be an object of charity. This I suppose to be false, unless it it supposed that nobody is a proper object of charity unless they have no estate left to live upon, which is very unreasonable, and what I have already shown to be false when I showed that it does not follow the rules of Christian charity to relieve only those who are reduced to extremity.

Nor do I suppose it was ever the intention of the law to cut off all occasion for Christian charity: nor is it fit there should be such a law. It is fit that the law should make provision for those who have no estates of their own; it is not fit that people who are reduced to that extremity should be left to be so precarious a supply as a voluntary charity. They are in extreme need of relief, and therefore it is fit that there should be something sure for them to depend on. But a voluntary charity in this corrupt world is an uncertain thing. Therefore the wisdom of the legislature did not think fit to leave those who are so reduced upon such a precarious foundation for subsistence. But I suppose not that it was ever the intention of the law to make provision for all that are in need, so as to leave no room for Christian charity.

The law does not actually relieve all cases of poverty

This objection is also built on another supposition which is equally false, namely that there are in fact no proper objects of charity but those that are relieved by the town. Let the intention of the law be what it will, yet if there are in fact people who are so needy as to be in need of our charity, then that law does not free us from the obligation to relieve them by our charity. For as we have just shown in answer to the last objection, if it is other people's responsibility more than ours to relieve them, we are still not free of responsibility if they do not do it. So if it is true that it is the town's *responsibility* to relieve all who are proper objects of charity, we are not excused if the town *in fact* does not do it.

If one of our neighbours suffers through the fault of a particular person, of a thief or robber, or of a town, it does not alter the case; but if he suffers and is without relief, it is an act of Christian charity in us to relieve him. Now it is too obvious to be denied that there are in fact people in such need that it would be a charitable act in us to help them, notwithstanding all that is done by the town. A man must hide his mental eyes to think otherwise.

A treatise concerning religious affections

Whom having not seen, ye love; in whom, though now ye see him not, yet believing, ye rejoice with joy unspeakable and full of glory (1 Peter 1:8)

Introduction

In these words, the apostle represents the state of the Christian to whom he wrote under persecutions. To these persecutions he refers in the two preceding verses, when he speaks of *the trial of their faith*, and of *their being in heaviness through manifold temptations*.

Such *trials* benefit true religion in three ways. The *truth* of it is manifested – it appears to be indeed *true religion*. Trials, above all other things, have a tendency to distinguish true religion and false, and to cause the difference between them to appear obvious. Hence they are called by the name of *trials*, in the verse preceding the text, and innumerable other places. They try the faith and religion of those who profess to be Christians, of what sort it is, just as what appears to be gold is tried in the fire, and it becomes clear whether it is true gold or not. And the faith of true Christians, being thus tried and proved to be true, is *found to praise, and honour, and glory*.

And then, these trials not only manifest the *truth* of true religion, but they make its genuine *beauty* and *amiableness* to appear remarkably. True virtue never appears so lovely as when it is most oppressed: and the divine excellence of real Christianity is never exhibited with such advantage as when it is under the greatest trials. It is then that true faith appears much more precious than gold; and upon this account it is *found to praise, and honour, and glory.*

Again, another benefit of such trials to true religion is that they purify and increase it. They not only show it to be *true,* but also tend to *refine* it, and deliver it from those mixtures of what is false, which encumber and impede it, so that nothing may be left but that which is true. They not only show the amiableness of true religion to the best advantage, but they tend to increase its beauty by establishing and confirming it from those things that obscured its lustre and glory. As gold that is tried in the fire is purged from its alloy, and all remainders of dross, and comes out more beautiful, so true faith, being tried as gold is tried in the fire, becomes more precious; and thus also is *found unto praise, and honour, and glory.* The apostle seems to refer to each of these benefits in the verse preceding the text.

And, in the text, the apostle observes how true religion *operated* in these Christians under their persecutions, by which these benefits appeared in them; or what manner of operation it was by which their religion, under persecution, was shown to be *true* religion in its genuine *beauty* and *amiableness,* and also appeared to be *increased* and *purified,* and so was likely to be *found unto praise, and honour, and glory, at the appearing of Jesus Christ.* And in the text the apostle notices two kinds of operation, or exercise of true religion, in them, under sufferings, in which these benefits appeared.

Love to Christ

Whom having not seen, ye love. The world was ready to wonder what strange principle it was that influenced them to expose themselves to such great sufferings, to forsake the things that were seen, and renounce all that was dear and pleasant, which was the object of sense. They seemed to the men of the world as if they were beside themselves; there was nothing in their view that could induce them to suffer like that, or to support them under and carry them through such trials. But although there was nothing that the world saw, or that the Christians themselves ever saw with their bodily eyes, that influenced and supported them like this, they still had a supernatural principle of love to something *unseen;* they loved Jesus Christ, for they saw him spiritually, when the world did not see him, and they themselves had never seen him with bodily eyes.

Joy in Christ

Though their outward sufferings were very grievous, their inward spiritual joys were greater than their sufferings; and these supported them, and enabled them to suffer with cheerfulness.

There are two things which the apostle takes notice of in the text concerning this joy.

The manner in which it arises

The way in which Christ, though unseen, is the foundation of this joy is by *faith,* which is the evidence of things not seen: *in whom, though now ye see him not, yet BELIEVING, ye rejoice.*

Its nature

This joy is *unspeakable, and full of glory.* It is *unspeakable* in *kind —* very different from worldly joys and carnal delights; of a vastly more pure, sublime, and heavenly nature, being something supernatural, and truly divine, and so ineffably excellent! There were no words to describe its sublimity and exquisite sweetness.

It is unspeakable also in *degree,* for God chose to give them this holy joy with a liberal hand, in their state of persecution.

Their joy was *full of glory.* Although the joy was unspeakable, and no words were sufficient to describe it, something might still be said of it, and no words more fit to represent its excellence than that it was *full of glory* or, as it is in the original, *glorified joy.* In rejoicing with this joy, their minds were filled, as it were, with a glorious brightness, and their natures were exalted and perfected. It was a most worthy, noble rejoicing, that did not corrupt and debase the mind as many carnal joys do; but it greatly beautified and dignified it. It was a prelibation of the joy of heaven, that raised their minds to a degree of heavenly blessedness; it filled their minds with the light of God's glory, and made themselves shine with some communication of that glory.

Hence the proposition or doctrine that I would raise from these words is this: true religion, in great part, consists in holy affections.

We see that the apostle, in remarking the operations and exercises of religion in these Christians, when it had its greatest trial by persecution, as gold is tried in the fire – and when it not only proved true, but was most pure from dross and admixtures – and when it appeared in them most in its genuine excellence and native beauty, and was found to praise, and honour, and glory – he singles out the religious affections of *love* and *joy* as those exercises in which their religion thus appeared *true, pure,* and *glorious.*

Here it may be inquired what the *affections* of the mind are. I answer that the affections are none other than the more vigorous and *conscious exercises of the inclination and will* of the soul.

God has endued the soul with two principal faculties: one, by which it is capable of *perception* and speculation, or by which it discerns and judges things – this is called the *understanding.* The other, that by which the soul is in some way *inclined* with respect to the things it views or considers: or it is the faculty by which the soul beholds things – not as an indifferent unaffected spectator, but either liking or disliking, pleased or displeased, approving or rejecting. This faculty is called by various names: it is sometimes called the *inclination*; and, as it relates to the actions determined and governed by it, the *will*; and the *mind,* with regard to the exercises of this faculty, is often called the *heart.*

The *exercises* of this last faculty are of two sorts; either those by which the soul is carried out towards the things in view in *approving* them, being pleased with and inclined to them; or, those in which the soul opposes the things in view, in *disapproving* them; and in being displeased with, averse from, and rejecting them. And as the exercises of the inclination are various in their *kinds,* so they are much more various in their *degrees.* There are some exercises of pleasedness or displeasedness, inclination or disinclination, in which the soul is carried little beyond a state of perfect indifference. And there are other degrees in which the approbation or dislike, pleasedness or aversion, are stronger; in which we may rise higher and higher, till the soul comes to act vigorously, and its actings are with such strength that (through the laws of union which the Creator has fixed between soul and body) the motion of the blood and animal spirits begins to be perceptibly altered, and some bodily sensation often arises, especially about the *heart* and vitals, which are the fountain of the fluids of the body. From this it comes to pass that the *mind,* with regard to the exercises of this faculty, perhaps in all nations and ages, is called the *heart*. And it is to be noted that they are these more vigorous and perceptible exercises of this faculty, which are called the *affections.*

The *will,* and the *affections* of the souls, are not two faculties; the affections are not essentially distinct from the will, nor do they differ from the mere *actings* of the will and inclination, but only in the liveliness and perceptibility of exercise. It must be confessed that language is here somewhat imperfect, the meaning of words in a considerable measure loose and unfixed, and not precisely limited by custom which governs the use of language. In some sense, the affection of the soul does not at all differ from the will and inclination, and the will is never in any exercise further than it is *affected*; it is not moved out of a state of perfect indifference in any other way than as it is *affected* one way or another. But yet there are many actings of the will and inclination that are not so commonly called *affections.* In everything we do in which we act voluntarily, there is an exercise of the will and inclination. It is our inclination that governs us in our actions; but *all the actings* of the inclination and will are not ordinarily called affections. Yet what are commonly called affections only differ from them essentially in the *degree* and *manner* of exercise. In every act of the will whatsoever, the soul either likes or dislikes, is either inclined or disinclined to, what is in view. These are not *essentially* different from the affections of *love* and *hatred*. A liking or inclination of the soul to a thing, if it is in a high degree vigorous and lively, is the very same thing as the affection of *love;* and a disliking and disinclining, if in a great degree, is the very same as *hatred*. In every act of the will *for* or *towards* something not present, the soul is in some degree *inclined* to that thing; and that inclination, if in a considerable degree, is the very same as the affection of *desire*. And in every degree of an act of the will in which the soul approves of something present, there is a degree of pleasedness; and that pleasedness, if it is in a considerable degree, is the very same as the affection of *joy* or *delight*. And if the will disapproves of what is present, the soul is in some degree displeased, and if that displeasedness is great, it is the very same as the affection of *grief* or *sorrow*.

Our nature, and the laws of the union of soul and body, seem to be such that there is never in any case whatsoever any lively and vigorous exercise of the inclination without some effect upon the body, in some alteration of the motion of its fluids, and especially of the animal spirits. And, on the other hand, from the same laws of union, over the constitution of the body and the motion of its fluids, may promote the exercise of the affections. But still, it is not the body, but only the mind that is the proper seat of the affections. The body of man is no more capable of being really the subject of love or hatred, joy or sorrow, fear or hope, than the body of a tree, or than the same body of man is capable of thinking and understanding. As it is only the soul that has ideas, so it is only the soul that is pleased or displeased with its ideas. As it is only the soul that thinks, so it is only the soul that loves or hates, rejoices or is grieved at, what it thinks of. Nor are these motions of the animal spirits and fluids of the body anything properly belonging to the *nature* of the affections (though they always *accompany* them, in the present state), but are only effects or concomitants of the affections, which are entirely distinct from the affections themselves, and no way essential to them; so that an unbodied spirit may be as capable of love and hatred, joy or sorrow, hope or fear, or other affections, as one that is united to a body.

The *affections* and *passions* are frequently spoken of as the same; and yet, in the more common use of speech, there is in some respect a difference. *Affection* is a word that, in its ordinary signification, seems to be something more extensive than *passion*, being used for all vigorous lively actings of the will or inclination; but *passion* is used for those that are more sudden, and whose effects on the animal spirits are more violent, the mind being more overpowered, and less in its own command.

As all the exercises of inclination and will are concerned either in approving and liking, or disapproving and rejecting, so the affections are of two sorts: they are those by which the soul is carried out to what is in view, cleaving *to* it, or *seeking* it; or those by which it is averse *from* it, and *opposes* it. Of the former sort are *love, desire, hope, joy, gratitude, complacence*. Of the latter kind are *hatred, fear, anger, grief*, and such like; which it is needless now to stop to define particularly.

And there are some affections in which there is a *combination* of each of the aforementioned kinds of actings of the will. For example, in the affection of *pity* there is something of the *former kind* towards the person suffering, and something of the *latter*, towards what he suffers. Similarly, in *zeal*, there is in it high *approbation* of some person or thing, together with vigorous *opposition* to what is conceived to be contrary to it.

Religion and the affections

True religion, in great part, consists in the affections.

We must be fervent

What has been said of the *nature* of the affections makes this evident, and may be sufficient, without adding anything further, to

135

put this matter out of doubt – for who will deny that true religion consists, in a great measure, in vigorous and lively actings of the *inclination* and *will* of the soul, or the fervent exercises of the *heart*? The religion which God requires, and will accept, does not consist in weak, dull and lifeless wishes, scarcely raising us above a state of indifference. God, in his word, greatly insists that we should be in good earnest, *fervent in spirit*, and our hearts vigorously engaged in religion: 'Be ye fervent in spirit, serving the Lord' (Romans 12:11). 'And now Israel, what doth the Lord they God require of thee, but to fear the Lord thy God, to walk in all his ways, and to love him, and to serve the Lord thy God with all thy heart, and with all thy soul?' (Deuteronomy 10:12). 'Hear, O Israel, the Lord our God is one Lord: and thou shalt love the Lord thy God with all thy heart, and with all thy soul, and with all thy might' (Deuteronomy 6:4-5). It is this fervent, vigorous engagedness of the heart in religion that is the fruit of a real circumcision of the heart, or true regeneration, and that has the promises of life: 'And the Lord thy God will circumcise thine heart, and the heart of thy seed, to love the Lord thy God with all thy heart, and with all thy soul, that thou mayest live' (Deuteronomy 30:6).

If we are not in good earnest in religion, and our wills and inclinations are not strongly exercised, we are nothing. The things of religion are so great that the exercises of our hearts cannot be suitable to their nature and importance unless they are lively and powerful. Vigour in the actings of our inclinations is requisite in nothing so much as in religion; and in nothing is lukewarmness so odious. True religion is evermore a powerful thing; and its power appears, first, in its exercises in the heart, its principal and original seat. Hence true religion is called the *power of godliness*, in distinction from external appearances, which are the *form* of it: 'Having a form of godliness, but denying the power of it' (2 Timothy 3:5). The Spirit of God, in those who have sound and solid religion, is a Spirit of powerful holy affection; and therefore God is said to have given 'the Spirit of power, and of love, and of a sound mind' (2 Timothy 1:7). And such people, when they receive the Spirit of

God in his sanctifying and saving influences, are said to be 'baptised with the Holy Ghost, and with fire', by reason of the power and fervour of those exercises which the Spirit of God excites in them, and by which *their hearts*, when grace is in exercise, may be said to *burn within them* (Luke 24:32).

The business of *religion* is, from time to time, compared to those *exercises* in which people have their hearts and strength greatly exercised and engaged, such as running, wrestling, or agonizing for a great prize or crown, and fighting with strong enemies that seek our lives, and warring as those who by violence take a city or kingdom. Though true grace has various degrees, and there are some who are mere babies in Christ, in whom the exercise of the inclination and will towards divine and heavenly things is comparatively weak, yet everyone who has the power of godliness has his inclinations and heart exercised towards God and divine things with such strength and vigour that these holy exercises prevail in him above all carnal or natural affections, and are effectual to overcome them. For every true disciple of Christ loves him 'above father or mother, wife and children, brethren and sisters, houses and lands; yea more than his own life'. Hence it follows that wherever true religion is, there are vigorous exercises of the inclination and will towards divine objects; but as we saw before, the vigorous, lively, and perceptible exercises of the will are not other than the *affections* of the soul.

Affections are the spring of actions

The Author of our nature has not only given us affections, but has made them very much the spring of actions. As the *affections* not only necessarily belong to the *human nature* but are a very *great part* of it, so (inasmuch as by regeneration people are renewed in the whole man) *holy affections* not only necessarily belong to *true religion*, but are a very great part of such religion. And as true religion is practical, and God has so constituted the human nature that the affections are very much the spring of people's actions, this also shows that true religion must consist very much in the affections.

Such is man's nature that he is very inactive unless he is influenced by either *love* or *hatred, desire, hope, fear,* or some other affection. These affections we see to be the moving springs in all the affairs of life, which engage men in all their pursuits; and especially in affairs in which they are earnestly engaged, and which they pursue with vigour. We see the world of mankind exceedingly busy and active; and their affections are the springs of motion: take away all *love* and *hatred,* all *hope* and *fear,* all *anger, zeal,* and affectionate *desire,* and the world would be, in a great measure, motionless and dead: there would be no such thing as activity amongst mankind, or any earnest pursuit whatsoever. It is affection that engages the covetous man, and him that is greedy for wordly profits; it is by the affections that the ambitious man is put forward in his pursuit of worldly glory; and the affections also actuate the voluptuous man, in his pleasure and sensual delights. The world continues from age to age, in a continual commotion and agitation, in pursuit of these things; but take away affection, and the *spring* of all this motion would be gone; the motion itself would cease. And just as in wordly things wordly affections are very much the spring of men's motions and action, so in religious matters the spring of their actions are very much religious affections: he that only has doctrinal knowledge and speculation, without affection, is never *engaged* in the business of religion.

Religion takes hold of us as we are affected

Nothing is more manifest *in fact* than that the things of religion take hold of men's souls no further than they *affect* them. There are multitudes who often hear the word of God, of things infinitely great and important, and which most nearly concern them, yet all seems to be wholly ineffectual upon them, and to make no alteration in their disposition or behaviour. The reason is, they are not *affected* with what they hear. There are many who often hear of the glorious perfections of God, his almighty power, boundless wisdom, infinite majesty, and that holiness by which he is of purer

138

eyes than to behold evil, and cannot look on iniquity; together with his infinite goodness and mercy. They hear of the great work of God's wisdom, power, and goodness, in which there appear the admirable manifestations of these perfections. They hear particularly of the unspeakable love of God and Christ, and what Christ has done and suffered. They hear of the great things of another world, of eternal misery, in bearing the fierceness and wrath of almighty God; and of endless blessedness and glory in the presence of God, and the enjoyment of his love. They also hear the peremptory commands of God, his gracious counsels and warnings, and the sweet invitations of the gospel. Yet they remain as before, with no perceptible alteration either in heart or practice, because they are not *affected* with what they hear. I am bold to assert that there never was any considerable change wrought in the mind or conversation of any person, by anything of a religious nature that ever he read, heard, or saw, who did not have his affections moved. Never was a natural man engaged earnestly to seek his salvation; never were any such brought to cry after wisdom, and lift up their voice for understanding, and to wrestle with God in prayer for mercy; and never was one humbled, and brought to the feet of God, from anything that ever he heard or imagined of his own unworthiness and deservings of God's displeasure; nor was ever one induced to fly for refuge to Christ, while his heart remained unaffected. Nor was there ever a saint awakened out of a cold, lifeless frame, or recovered from a declining state in religion, and brought back from a lamentable departure from God, without having his heart affected. And, in a word, there never was anything considerable brought to pass in the heart or life of anyone living, by the things of religion, that had not his heart deeply affected by those things.

The Scriptures place religion in the affections

The Holy Scriptures everywhere place religion very much in the affections, such as fear, hope, love, hatred, desire, joy, sorrow, gratitude, compassion, and zeal.

Fear

The Scriptures place much of religion in godly fear – an experience of it is often spoken of as the character of those who are truly religious persons. *They tremble at God's word, they fear before him, their flesh trembles for fear of him, they are afraid of his judgements, his excellence makes them afraid, and his dread falls upon them*, etc. A name commonly given the saints in Scripture is *fearers of God*, or those that *fear the Lord*. And because this is a great part of true godliness, hence true godliness in general is very commonly called *the fear of God*.

Hope

Hope in God, and in the promises of his word, is often spoken of in the Scriptures as a very considerable part of true religion. It is mentioned as one of the three great things of which religion consists (1 Corinthians 13:13). Hope in the Lord is also frequently mentioned as the character of the saints: 'Happy is he that hath the God of Jacob for his help, whose *hope* is in the Lord his God' (Psalm 96:5). 'Be of good courage, and he shall strengthen your heart, all ye that *hope* in the Lord' (Psalm 31:24). And similarly in many other passages. Religious fear and hope are, once and again, joined together as jointly constituting the character of the true saints: 'Behold, the eye of the Lord is upon them that *fear* him, upon them that *hope* in his mercy' (Psalm 33:18). Hope is so great a part of true religion that the apostle says *we are saved by HOPE* (Romans 8:24). And this is spoken of as the *helmet* of the Christian soldier – 'and for an helmet, the *hope* of salvation' (1 Thessalonians 5:8) – and the sure and steadfast *anchor* of the soul, which preserves it from being cast away by the storms of this evil world: 'Which *hope* we have as an anchor of the soul, both sure and steadfast, and which entereth into that within the vail' (Hebrews 6:19). It is spoken of as a great benefit which true saints receive by Christ's resurrection: 'Blessed be the God and Father of our Lord Jesus Christ, which, according to his abundant mercy, hath begotten us again unto a lively *hope*, by the resurrection of Jesus Christ from the dead' (1 Peter 1:3).

Love and hatred

The Scriptures place religion very much in the affection of *love* – love to God, and the Lord Jesus Christ; love to the people of God, and to mankind. The texts in which this is clear, both in the Old Testament and the New, are innumerable. But of this more afterwards. The contrary affection of *hatred* also, as having sin for its object, is spoken of in Scripture as no inconsiderable part of true religion. It is spoken of as that by which true religion may be known and distinguished: 'The fear of the Lord is to *hate* evil' (Proverbs 8:13). Accordingly, the saints are called upon to give evidence of their sincerity by this: 'Ye that love the Lord, *hate* evil' (Psalm 97:10). And the psalmist often mentions it as an evidence of his sincerity: 'I will walk within my house with a perfect heart. I will set no wicked thing before mine eyes: I *hate* the work of them that turn aside' (Psalm 101:2-3). 'I *hate* every false way' (Psalm 119:104; also verse 128). Again: 'Do I not *hate* them, O Lord, that hate thee?' (Psalm 139:21).

Desire

Similarly, holy desire, exercised in longings, hungerings, and thirstings after God and holiness, is often mentioned in Scripture as an important part of true religion: 'The *desire* of our soul is to thy name, and to the remembrance of thee' (Isaiah 26:8). 'One thing have I *desired* of the Lord, and that will I seek after, that I may dwell in the house of the Lord all the days of my life; to behold the beauty of the Lord, and to inquire in his temple' (Psalm 27:4). 'As the heart panteth after the water-brooks, so panteth my soul after thee, O God. My soul *thirsteth* for God, for the living God: when shall I come and appear before God?' (Psalm 42:1-2). 'My soul *thirsteth* for thee, my flesh *longeth* for thee, in a dry and thirsty land where no water is: to see thy power and thy glory, so as I have seen thee in the sanctuary' (Psalm 63:1-2). 'How amiable are thy tabernacles, O Lord of hosts! My soul longeth, yea, even fainteth for the courts of the Lord: my heart and my flesh crieth out for the living God' (Psalm 84:1-2). 'My soul breaketh for the *longing* that it hath unto thy judgements at all times' (Psalm 119:20). Such a holy desire, or thirst of soul, denotes a man *truly blessed*: 'Blessed are they that do hunger and thirst after righteousness: for they shall be filled' (Matthew 5:6). And this holy thirst is connected with the blessings of *eternal life*: 'I will give unto him that is *athirst*, of the fountain of the water of life freely' (Revelation 21:6).

Joy

The Scriptures speak of holy *joy* as a great part of true religion. So it is represented in the text. And as an important part of religion, it is often pressed with great earnestness: *'Delight* thyself in the Lord; and he shall give thee the desires of thine heart' (Psalm 37:4). *'Rejoice* in the Lord, ye righteous' (Psalm 97:12; see also Psalm 33:1). *'Rejoice*, and be exceeding glad' (Matthew 5:12). 'Finally, brethren, *rejoice* in the Lord' (Philippians 3:1). *'Rejoice* in the Lord alway: and again I say, *rejoice'* (Philippians 4:4). *'Rejoice* evermore' (1 Thessalonians 5:16). 'Let Israel *rejoice* in him that made him: let the children of Israel be *joyful* in their King' (Psalm 149:2). This is mentioned among the principal fruits of the Spirit of grace: 'The fruit of the Spirit is love, *joy,* . . .' (Galatians 5:22). The psalmist mentions his holy joy as an evidence of his sincerity: 'I have *rejoiced* in the way of thy testimonies, as much as in all riches' (Psalm 119:14).

Sorrow

Religious sorrow, mourning, and brokenness of heart are also frequently spoken of as a great part of true religion. These things are often mentioned as distinguishing qualities of the true saints, and a great part of their character: 'Blessed are they that *mourn*: for they shall be comforted' (Matthew 5:4). 'The Lord is nigh unto them that are of a *broken heart*; and saveth such as be of a *contrite* spirit' (Psalm 34:18). 'The Lord hath anointed me . . . to bind up the brokenhearted . . . to comfort all that *mourn*' (Isaiah 61:1-2). This godly sorrow and brokenness of heart is often spoken of, not only as a distinguishing characteristic of the saints, but as that in them which is peculiarly acceptable and pleasing to God: 'The sacrifices of God are a broken spirit: a broken and a contrite heart, O God, thou wilt not despise' (Psalm 51:17). 'Thus saith the high and lofty One that inhabiteth eternity, whose name is holy, I dwell in the high and holy place; with him also that is of a contrite and humble spirit, to revive the spirit of the humble, and to revive the heart of the contrite ones' (Isaiah 57:15). 'To this man will I look, even to him that is poor and of a contrite spirit' (Isaiah 66:2).

Gratitude

Another affection often mentioned as that in whose exercise much of true religion appears, is gratitude – especially as exercised in thankfulness and praise to God. This being so much spoken of in the book of Psalms, and other parts of the Holy Scriptures, I need not mention particular texts.

Compassion

Again, the Holy Scriptures frequently speak of compassion or mercy as a very great and essential thing in true religion. A *merciful* man and a *good* man are equivalent terms in Scriptures: 'The righteous perisheth, and no man layeth it to heart; and *merciful men* are taken away' (Isaiah 57:1). And the Scripture chooses out this quality as that by which, in a special way, the righteous man is deciphered: 'The *righteous* showeth *mercy,* and giveth . . . . He is ever *merciful,* and lendeth' (Psalm 37:21, 26). 'He that honoureth the Lord, hath *mercy* on the poor' (Proverbs 14:31). 'Put ye on, as the elect of God, holy and beloved, *bowels of mercies*' (Colossians 3:12). This is one of those great things by which the truly blessed are described by our Saviour: 'Blessed are the merciful: for they shall obtain mercy' (Matthew 5:7). And Christ also speaks of this as one of the weightier matters of the law: 'Woe unto you, scribes and Pharisees, hypocrites! for ye pay tithe of mint, and anise, and cummin, and have omitted the weightier matters of the law, judgement, *mercy,* and faith' (Matthew 23:23). Micah 6:8 says the same thing: 'He hath showed thee, O man, what is good: and what doth the Lord require of thee, but to do justice, and love *mercy,* and walk humbly with thy God?' And also Hosea 6:6: 'For I desired *mercy,* and not sacrifice' – a text much delighted in by our Saviour, as appears from his citing it repeatedly (Matthew 9:13; 12:7).

Zeal

Zeal is also spoken of as a very essential part of the religion of true saints. This was a great thing which Christ had in view, in giving himself for our redemption: 'Who gave himself for us, that he might redeem us from all iniquity, and purify unto himself a peculiar people, *zealous* of good works' (Titus 2:14). And this was the great thing lacking in the lukewarm Laodiceans (Revelation 3:15-19).

I have mentioned just a few texts out of an innumerable multitude which place religion very much in the affections. But what has been observed may be sufficient to show that those who maintain the contrary must throw away what we have usually claimed for our Bible, and get some other rule by which to judge the nature of religion.

True religion is comprehended in love

The Scriptures represent true religion as being summarily comprehended in love, the chief of the affections, and the fountain of all others. Thus our blessed Saviour represents the matter in answer to the lawyer who asked him which was the great commandment of the law (Matthew 22:37-40): 'Jesus said unto him, Thou shalt love the Lord thy God with all thy heart, and with all thy soul, and with all thy mind. This is the first and great commandment. And the second is like unto it, Thou shalt love thy neighbour as thyself. On these two commandments hang all the law and the prophets.' These two commandments comprehend all the duty prescribed in the law and the prophets. And the apostle Paul puts it the same way: 'He that loveth another, hath fulfilled the law . . . Love is the fulfilling of the law' (Romans 13:8,10). 'For all the law is fulfilled in one word, even in this, Thou shalt love thy neighbour as thyself' (Galatians 5:14). Now the end of the commandment is charity, out of a pure heart' (1 Timothy 1:5). The same apostle speaks of love as the greatest thing in religion, as the essence and soul of it; without which, the greatest knowledge and gifts, the most glaring profession, and everything else which appertains to religion, are vain and worthless. He also represents it as the *fountain* from which comes all that is good (1 Corinthians 13, throughout – for the word which is there rendered *charity* is in the original *agape*, the proper English of which is *love*).

Now although it is true that the love thus spoken of includes the whole of a sincerely benevolent propensity of the soul towards God and man, yet it is evident from what has been observed before that this propensity or inclination of the soul, when in perceptible and vigorous exercise, becomes *affection*, and is no other than affectionate love. And surely it is such vigorous and fervent love that Christ represents as the sum of all religion, when he speaks of loving God with *all our hearts*, with *all our souls*, and with *all our minds*, and our neighbour as ourselves.

Indeed, it cannot be supposed, when this affection of love is spoken of as the sum of all religion, that it means the act without the habit, or that the exercise of the understanding is excluded, which is implied in all rational affection. But it is doubtless true, and evident from the Scriptures, that the *essence* of all true religion lies in holy love; and that in this divine affection – and habitual disposition to it, that light which is the foundation of it, and those things which are its fruits – consists the *whole* of religion.

Hence it clearly and certainly appears that great part of true religion consists in the affections. For love is not only of the affections, but it is the first and chief of them, and the fountain of all the others. From love arises hatred of those things which are contrary to what we love, or which oppose and thwart us in those things that we delight in: and from the various exercises of love and hatred, according to the circumstances of the objects of those affections, as present or absent, certain or uncertain, probable or improbable, arise all those other affections of *desire, hope, fear, joy, grief, grati-tude, anger*, etc. From a vigorous, affectionate, and fervent *love to God*, other *religious* affections will necessarily arise; hence will arise an intense *hatred* and *fear* of sin; a *dread* of God's displeasure; *grat-itude* to God for his goodness; *pleasure* and *joy* in God when he is graciously and perceptibly present; *grief* when he is absent; a joyful *hope* when a future enjoyment of God is expected; and fervent *zeal* for the divine glory. Similarly, from a fervent *love to men* will arise all other virtuous affections towards them.

The saints displayed holy affections

The religion of the most eminent saints of whom we have an account in Scripture consisted much in holy affections. I shall take particular notice of three eminent saints who have expressed the frame and sentiments of their own hearts, described their own reli-gion, and the manner of their fellowship with God, in the writings which they have left us, and which are a part of the sacred canon.

David

The first instance is David, that *man after God's own heart*, who has given us a lively picture of his religion in the book of Psalms. These holy songs are nothing else but the expressions and breathings of devout and holy affections, such as a humble and fervent *love* to God, *admiration* of his glorious perfections and wonderful works, earnest *desires*, thirstings, and pantings of soul after him; *delight* and *joy* in God, a sweet and melting *gratitude* for his great good-ness, a holy *exultation* and triumph of soul in his favour, sufficiency, and faithfulness; his *love* to, and *delight* in, the saints, the excellent of the earth, his great *delight* in the word and ordinances of God, his *grief* for his own and other's sins, and his fervent *zeal* for God, and against the enemies of God and his church. And these expres-sions of holy affection of which the Psalms of David are everywhere full, are the more to our present purpose because those psalms are not only the expressions of the religion of so eminent a saint, but

146

were also, by the direction of the Holy Spirit, penned for the use of the church of God in its public worship, not only in that age, but in later times, as being fitted to express the religion of all saints, in all ages, as well as the religion of the psalmist. And it is moreover noticeable that David, in the book of Psalms, speaks not as a private individual, but as the Psalmist of Israel, as the subordinate head of the church of God and leader in their worship and praises; and in many of the psalms he speaks in the name of Christ, as personating him in these breathings forth of holy affections; and in many others he speaks in the name of the church.

Paul

Another instance I shall observe is the apostle Paul, who was in many respects the chief of all the ministers of the New Testament, being above all others a vessel chosen for Christ, to bear his name before the Gentiles. He was made the chief instrument of propagating and establishing the Christian church in the world, and of distinctly revealing the glorious mysteries of the gospel, for the instruction of the church in all ages; and (as not improbably thought by some) was the most eminent servant of Christ that ever lived, and received the highest rewards in the heavenly kingdom in his Master. By what is said of him in the Scripture, he appears to have been a person full of affection; and it is very clear that the religion he expresses in his letters consisted very much in holy affections. It appears from all his expressions of himself that he was, in the course of his life, inflamed, actuated, and entirely swallowed up by a most ardent *love* to his glorious Lord, esteeming all things as loss for the excellence of the knowledge of him, and esteeming them but dung that he might win him. He represents himself as overpowered by this holy affection, and as it were compelled by it to go forward in his service, through all difficulties and sufferings (2 Corinthians 5:14-15). And his letters are full of expressions of an overflowing affection towards the people of Christ: he speaks of his *dear love* to them (2 Corinthians 12:19; Philippians 4:1-2; 2 Timothy 1:2), of his *abundant love* (2 Corinthians 2:4) and of his *affectionate and tender love*, like that of a nurse towards her children: 'But we were gentle among you, even as a nurse cherisheth her children: so, being affectionately desirous of you, we were willing to have imparted unto you, not the gospel of God only, but also our own souls, because ye were dear unto us' (1 Thessalonians 2:7-8). So also he speaks of his *bowels of love* (Philippians 1:8; Philemon 5, 12, 20), of his *earnest care* for others (2 Corinthians 8:16), of his *bowels of pity* or *mercy* towards them (Philippians 2:1), and of his concern for others, even to *anguish of heart*: 'For out of much affliction and anguish of heart, I wrote unto you with many tears; not that you should be grieved, but that ye might know the love which I have more abundantly unto you' (2 Corinthians 2:4). He speaks of the *great conflict* of his soul for them (Colossians 2:1) and of *great and continual grief* he had *in his heart* from *compassion* to the Jews (Romans 10:2). He speaks of his *mouth being opened, and his heart enlarged* towards Christians: 'O ye Corinthians, our mouth is open unto you, our heart is enlarged' (2 Corinthians 6:11). He often speaks of his *affectionate and longing desires* (1 Thessalonians 2:8; Romans 1:11, Philippians 1:8 and 4:1-2; 2 Timothy 1:4).

The same apostle very often, in his letters, expresses the affection of *joy* (2 Corinthians 1:12; 7:7; 9:16; Philippians 1:4; 2:1-2; 3:3; Colossians 1:24; 1 Thessalonians 3:9). He speaks of his rejoicing *with great joy* (Philippians 4:10; Philemon 1:7), of his *joying and rejoicing* (Philippians 2:1, 7), of his *rejoicing exceedingly* (2 Corinthians 7:13), being *filled with comfort, exceeding joyful* (2 Corinthians 7:4), and *always rejoicing* (2 Corinthians 6:10). So he speaks of the *triumphs* of his soul (2 Corinthians 2:14) and of his *glorying in tribulation* (2 Thessalonians 1:4; Romans 5:3). In Philippians 1:20 he speaks of his *earnest expectation*, and his *hope*. He likewise expresses an affection of *godly jealousy* (2 Corinthians 11:2-3). And it appears from the whole story of his life after his conversion that the affection of *zeal*, having the cause of his Master and the interest and prosperity of his church for its object, was mighty in him, continually inflaming his heart, strongly engaging to great and constant labours in instructing, exhorting, warning,

148

and reproving others, *travailing in birth with them*; conflicting with those powerful and innumerable enemies who continually opposed him, wrestling with principalities and powers, not fighting as one who beats the air, running the race set before him, continually pressing forwards through all manner of difficulties and sufferings; so that others thought him quite beside himself. And how full he was of affection further appears by his being so full of tears: in 2 Corinthians 2:4 and Acts 20:19 he speaks of his *many tears*, and in Acts 20:31 of his *tears* that he shed *continually, night and day*.

Now if anyone can consider these accounts given in the Scriptures of this great apostle, and which he gives of himself, and yet not see that his religion consisted much in *affection*, he must have a strange faculty of managing his eyes in order to shut out the light which shines most full in his face.

John

The other instance I shall mention is that of the apostle John, the beloved disciple, who was the nearest and dearest to his Master of any of the twelve, and who was by him admitted to the greatest privileges of any of them. He was not only one of the three who were admitted to be present with him on the mount at his transfiguration, and at the raising of Jairus's daughter, and whom he took with him when he was in his agony, and one of three spoken of by the apostle Paul as the three main pillars of the Christian church; but he was favoured above all in being admitted to lean on his Master's bosom at his last supper, and in being chosen by Christ as the disciple to whom he would reveal his wonderful dispensations towards his church, to the end of time. By him the canon of the New Testament, and of the whole Scripture, was shut up, and he was preserved much longer than all the rest of the apostles, to set all things in order in the Christian church after their death.

It is evident from all his writings that he was a person remarkably full of affection: his addresses to those whom he wrote to being inexpressibly tender and full of feeling, breathing nothing but the most fervent *love*, as though he were all made up of sweet and holy affection. The proofs of this cannot be given without disadvantage, unless we should transcribe his whole writings.

Christ himself was tenderhearted

He whom God sent into the world to be the light of the world and the head of the whole church, and the perfect example of true religion and virtue for the imitation of all, the Shepherd whom the whole flock should follow wherever he goes – the Lord Jesus Christ – was of a remarkably tender and affectionate heart; and his virtue was expressed very much in the exercise of holy affections. He was the greatest instance of ardent, vigorous, and strong *love*, to both God and man, that ever was. It was these affections which got the victory in that mighty struggle and conflict of his affections, in his agonies, when *he prayed more earnestly, and offered strong crying and tears*, and wrestled in tears and in blood. Such was the power of the exercises of his holy love that they were stronger than death, and in that great struggle overcame those strong exercises of the natural affections of fear and grief, when his soul was exceeding sorrowful, even unto death.

He also appeared to be full of affection in the course of his life. We read of his great *zeal*, fulfilling the expression in Psalm 60: 'The zeal of thine house hath eaten me up' (John 2:17). We read of his *grief* for the sins of men: 'He looked round about on them with anger, being grieved for the hardness of their hearts' (Mark 3:5). And we read of his breaking out in tears and exclamations, thinking about the sin and misery of ungodly men, and at the sight of the city of Jerusalem, which was full of such inhabitants: 'And when he was come near, he beheld the city, and wept over it, saying, If thou hadst known, even thou, at least in this thy day, the things which belong unto thy peace! but now they are hid from thine eyes' (Luke 19:41-42). 'O Jerusalem, Jerusalem, which killest the prophets and stonest them that are sent unto thee: how often would I have gathered thy children together, as a hen doth gather her brood under her wings, and ye would not!' (Luke 13:34). We read of Christ's earnest *desire*: 'With desire have I desired to eat this passover with you before I suffer' (Luke 22:15). We often read of the affection of *pity* or *compassion* in Christ (Matthew 15:32 and 18:34; Luke 7:13), and of his being *moved with compassion* (Matthew 9:36 and 14:14; Mark 6:34). And how tender did his heart appear to be on the occasion of Mary's and Martha's mourning for their brother, and coming to him with their complaints and tears! Their tears soon drew tears from his eyes; he was affected with their grief, and *wept* with them; though he knew their sorrow would soon be turned into joy by their brother being raised from the dead: see John 11. And how ineffably affectionate was that last and dying discourse which Jesus had with his eleven disciples the evening before he was crucified – when he told them he was going away, and foretold the great difficulties and sufferings they would meet with in the world, when he had gone; and comforted and counselled them, as his dear little children; and bequeathed to them his Holy Spirit, and therein his peace, his comfort and joy, as it were in his last will and testament (John 13-16); and concluded the whole with that affectionate intercessory prayer for them, and his whole church, in chapter 17. Of all the discourses ever penned or uttered by the mouth of any man, this seems to be the most affectionate and affecting.

The religion of heaven consists very much in affection

There is doubtless true religion in heaven, and true religion in its utmost purity and perfection. But according to the scriptural representation of the heavenly state, the religion of heaven consists chiefly in holy and mighty *love* and *joy*, and the expression of these in most fervent and exalted praises. So the religion of the saints in heaven consists in the same things as that religion of the saints on earth which is spoken of in our text, namely *love*, and *joy unspeakable, and full of glory*. Now it would be very foolish to pretend that because the saints in heaven are not united to flesh and blood, and have no animal fluids to be moved (through the laws of union of soul and body) with those great emotions of their souls, that there-

151

fore their exceeding love and joy are not affections. We are not speaking of the affections of the body, but those of the soul, the chief of which are *love* and *joy*. When these are in the soul, whether that be in the body or out of it, the soul is affected and moved. And when they are in the soul, in that strength in which they are in the saints in heaven, it is mightily affected and moved, or, which is the same thing, has great affections. It is true, we do not experimentally know what love and joy are in a soul out of the body, or in a glorified body; i.e. we have not had experience of love and joy in a soul in these circumstances; but the saints on earth do know that love and joy are of the same kind as the love and joy which are in heaven, in separate souls there. The love and joy of the saints on earth is the beginning and dawning of the light, life, and blessedness of heaven, and is like their love and joy there; or rather, the same in nature, though not the same in degree and circumstances. It is unreasonable therefore to suppose that the love and joy of the saints in heaven differ not only in degree and circumstances from the holy love and joy of the saints on earth, but also in nature, so that they are not affections; and merely because they have no blood and animal spirits to be set in motion by them. The motion of the blood and animal spirits is not of the *essence* of these affections in men on the earth, but the *effect* of them; although by their reaction they may make some circumstantial difference in the sensation of the mind. There is a sensation of the *mind* which loves and rejoices, *antecedent* to any effects on the fluids of the body; and therefore, does not depend on these motions on the body, and so may be in the soul without the body. And wherever there are the exercises of love and joy, there is that sensation of the mind, whether it be in the body or out; and that inward sensation, or kind of spiritual feeling, is what is called affection. The soul, when it is thus moved, is said to be *affected*, and especially when this inward sensation and motion are to a very high degree, as they are in the saints in heaven. If we can learn anything of the state of heaven from Scripture, the love and joy that the saints have there is exceedingly great and vigourous, impressing the heart with the strongest and most lively sensation of inexpressible sweetness, mightily moving, animating, and engaging them, making them like a flame of fire. And if such love and joy are not affections, then the word *affection* is of no use in language. Will anyone say that the saints in heaven, in beholding the face of their Father and the glory of their Redeemer, in contemplating his wonderful works, and particularly his laying down his life for them, have their hearts nothing moved and affected by all which they behold or consider?

Hence, therefore, the religion of heaven, being full of holy love and joy, consists very much in affection; and therefore, undoubtedly, true religion consists very much in affection. The way to learn the true nature of anything is to go where that thing is to be found in its purity and perfection. If we would know the nature of true gold, we must view it not in the ore but when it is refined. If we want to learn what true religion is, we must go where there is true religion, and nothing but true religion, and in its highest perfection, without any defect or mixture. All who are truly religious are not of this world; they are strangers here, and belong to heaven; they are born from above; heaven is their native country, and the nature which they receive by this heavenly birth is a heavenly nature. They receive *an anointing from above*; that principle of true religion which is in them is a communication of the religion of heaven; their grace is the dawn of glory; and God fits them for that world by conforming them to it.

The means and expressions of true religion

This appears from the nature and design of the ordinances and duties which God has appointed as means and expressions of true religion.

Prayer

To instance the duty of prayer: it is clear that we are not appointed, in this duty, to declare God's perfections, his majesty, holiness, goodness, and all sufficiency, our own meanness, emptiness, dependence, and unworthiness, our wants and desires – in order to inform God of these things, or to incline his heart and prevail with him to be willing to show us mercy. Rather, it is to affect our own hearts with the things we express, and so to prepare us to receive the blessings we ask. And such gestures and manner of external behaviour in the worship of God, which custom has made to express humility and reverence, can only be of use as they have some tendency to *affect* our own hearts, or the hearts of others.

Singing

The duty of singing praises to God seems to be appointed wholly to excite and express religious affections. No other reason can be given why we should express ourselves to God in verse, rather than in prose, and do it with music, except that such is our nature and frame that these things have a tendency to move our affections.

Sacraments

The same thing appears in the nature and design of the *sacraments,* which God has appointed. God, considering our frame, has not only appointed that we should be told of the great things of the gospel and the redemption of Christ, and be instructed in them by his word; but also that they should be, as it were, exhibited to our view in perceptible representations, so that we are the more affected by them.

Preaching

The impressing of divine things on the hearts and affections of men is evidently one great end for which God has ordained that his word delivered in the Holy Scriptures should be explained, applied, and driven home in preaching. Therefore it does not answer the aim which God in this institution, merely for men to have good commentaries and expositions of the Scripture, and other good books of divinity; because, although these may tend, as well as preaching, to give a good doctrinal or speculative understanding of the word of God, yet they do not have an equal tendency to impress them on men's hearts and affections. God has appointed a particular and lively application of his word, in the preaching of it, as a fit means to affect sinners with the importance of religion, their own misery, the necessity of a remedy, and the glory and sufficiency of a remedy provided; to stir up the pure minds of the saints, quicken their affections by often bringing the great things of religion to their remembrance, and setting them in their proper colours, though they know them, and have been fully instructed in them already (2 Peter 1:12-13). And particularly, to promote those two affections in them, which are spoken of in the text, *love* and *joy*: 'Christ gave some, apostles; and some, prophets; and some, evangelists; and some, pastors and teachers; that the body of Christ might be edified in love' (Ephesians 4:11-12, 16). The apostle in instructing and counselling Timothy concerning the work of the ministry, informs him that the great end of that word which a minister is to preach is *love* or *charity* (1 Timothy 1:3-5). And God has appointed preaching as a means to promote joy in the saints; therefore minsters are called *helpers of their joy* (2 Corinthians 1:24).

Hardness of heart

It is an evidence that true religion lies very much in the affections, that the Scriptures place the sin of the heart very much in *hardness of heart*. It was hardness of heart which excited grief and displeasure in Christ towards the Jews: 'He looked round about on them with anger, being grieved for the hardness of their hearts' (Mark 3:5). It is from men's having such a heart as this that they treasure up wrath for themselves: 'After thy hardness and impenitent heart, treasurest up unto thyself wrath against the day of wrath, and revelation of the righteous judgement of God' (Romans 2:5). The reason given why the house of Israel would not obey God was that they were hardhearted: 'But the house of Israel will not hearken unto thee; for they will not hearken unto me; for all the house of Israel are impudent and hardhearted' (Ezekiel 3:7). The wickedness of that perverse rebellious generation in the wilderness is ascribed to the hardness of their hearts: 'Today if ye will hear my voice, harden not your heart, as in the provocation, and as in the day of temptation in the wilderness; when your fathers tempted me, proved me, and saw my work: forty years long was I grieved with this generation, and said, it is a people that do err in their heart . . .' (Psalm 95:7-10). This is spoken of as what prevented Zedekiah's turning to the Lord: 'He stiffened his neck, and hardened his heart from turning to the Lord God of Israel' (2 Chronicles 36:13). This principle is that from which men are without the fear of God, and depart from his ways: 'O Lord, why hast thou made us to err from thy ways? and hardened our heart from thy fear?' (Isaiah 63:17). And men rejecting Christ, and opposing Christianity, are charged with this principle: 'But divers were hardened, and believed not, but spake evil of that way before the multitude' (Acts 19:9). God's leaving men to the power of the sin and corruption of the heart is often expressed by his hardening their hearts: 'Therefore hath he mercy on whom he will have mercy, and whom he will he hardeneth' (Romans 9:18). 'He hath blinded their minds, and hardened their hearts' (John 12:40). And the apostle seems to speak of *an evil heart, that departs from the living God* as the same thing as a *hard heart*: 'Harden not your heart, as in the provocation. . . . Take heed, therefore, lest there be in any of you an evil heart of unbelief, in departing from the living God: but exhort one another daily while it is called to-day; lest any of you be hardened through the deceitfulness of sin' (Hebrews 3:8, 12-13). And that great work of God in conversion, which consists in delivering a person from the power of sin, and mortifying corruption, is expressed again and again by God's taking away the heart of stone, and giving a heart of flesh (Ezekiel 11:19 and 36:26).

Now, by a *hard* heart is plainly meant an *unaffected* heart, or a heart not easy to be moved with virtuous affections, like a stone, insensitive, stupid, unmoved, and hard heart, and is opposed to a *heart of flesh*, that has feeling, and is touched and moved. We read in Scripture of a *hard heart* and a *tender heart*, and doubtless we are to understand these as contrary to one another. But what is a tender heart but a heart which is easily impressed with what ought to affect it? God commends Josiah because his heart was tender, and it is evident from those things which are mentioned as expressions and evidences of this tenderness of heart that it means his heart being easily moved with religious and pious affections: 'Because thine heart was tender, and thou hast humbled thyself before the Lord, when thou heardst what I spake against this place, and against the inhabitants thereof, that they should become a desolation and a curse, and hast rent thy clothes, and went before me, I also have heard thee, saith the Lord' (2 Kings 22:19). And this is one thing in which it is necessary we should become as little children, in order to enter into the kingdom of God – that we should have our hearts tender, and easily affected and moved in spiritual and divine things, as little children have in other things.

It is very plain in some passages that by hardness of heart is meant a heart void of affection. So, to signify the ostrich's being without natural affection to her young, it is said: 'She hardeneth her heart against her young ones, as though they were not hers' (Job 39:16). So a person having a heart unaffected in time of danger is expressed by his hardening his heart: 'Happy is the man that feareth alway; but he that hardeneth his heart, shall fall into mischief' (Proverbs 28:14).

Now, therefore, since it is so plain that by a hard heart Scripture means a heart destitute of pious affections, and since also the Scriptures so frequently place the sin and corruption of the heart in its hardness, it is evident that the grace and holiness of the heart, on the contrary, must in a great measure consists in its having pious affections, and being easily susceptible to such affections. Theologians are generally agreed that sin radically and fundamentally consists in what is negative, or privative, having its root and foundation in a privation or lack of holiness. And therefore, undoubtedly, if sin very much consists in hardness of heart, and so in the lack of pious affections, holiness consists very much in those pious affections.

I am far from supposing that all affections manifest a tender heart; hatred, anger, vainglory, and other selfish and self-exalting affections may greatly prevail in the hardest heart. But yet it is evident that *hardness of heart* and *tenderness of heart* are expressions that relate to the affections of the heart, and denote its being susceptible to, or shut up against, certain affections, of which I shall have occasion to speak more afterwards.

Without holy affection, there is no true religion

On the whole, I think it clearly and abundantly evident that true religion lives very much in the affections. Not that I think these arguments prove that religion in the hearts of the truly godly is ever in exact proportion to the degree of affection and present emotion of the mind: for, undoubtedly, there is much affection in the true saints which is not spiritual; their religious affections are often mixed; all is not from grace, but much from nature. And though the affections do not have their seat in the body, yet the constitution of the body may very much contribute to the present emotion of the mind. The degree of religion is to be estimated by the fixedness and strength of habit exercised in affection, whereby holy affection is habitual, rather than by the degree of the present exercise; and the strength of that habit is not always in proportion to outward effects and manifestations, or indeed inward ones, in the hurry, vehemence, and sudden changes of the course of the thoughts. But yet it is evident that religion consists so much in the affections that without holy affection there is no true religion. No light in the understanding is good if it does not produce holy affection in the heart; no habit or principle in the heart is good if it has no such exercise; and no external fruit is good if it does not proceed from such exercises.

Some inferences from the doctrine

The error of discarding religious affections

From this we may learn how great is the error of those who are for discarding all religious affections as having nothing solid or substantial in them. There seems to be too much of a disposition this way prevailing at this time. Because many who, in the recent extraordinary time, appeared to have great religious affections, did not manifest a right temper of mind, and run into many errors in the heat of their zeal; and because the high affections of many seem to have come to nothing so soon, and some who seemed to be mightily raised and swallowed with joy and zeal for a while seem to have returned like the dog to his vomit – therefore religious affections in general have become discredited with great numbers, as though true religion did not consist in them at all. Thus we easily and naturally run from one extreme to another. A little while ago we were in the other extreme: there was a prevalent disposition to look upon all high religious affections as eminent exercises of true grace, without much inquiry into the nature and source of those affections, and the manner in which they arose. If people only appeared to be indeed very much moved and raised, so as to be full of religious talk, and express themselves with great warmth and earnestness, and to be *filled*, or to be *very full*, as the phrases were, it was too much the manner, without further examination, to conclude such persons were full of the Spirit of God, and had eminent experience of his gracious influences. This was the extreme which was prevailing three or four years ago. But of late, instead of esteeming and admiring all religious affections, without distinction, it is much more prevalent to reject and discard all without distinction. In this we see the subtlety of Satan. While he saw that affections were much in vogue, knowing the greater part were not versed in such things, and had not had much experience of great religious affections, enabling them to judge well, and to distinguish between true and false, then he knew he could best play his game by sowing tares among the wheat, and mingling false affections with the works of God's Spirit. He knew this to be a likely way to delude and eternally ruin many souls, and entangle them in a dreadful wilderness, and by and by to bring all religion into disrepute.

But now, then the ill consequences of these false affections appear, and it has become very apparent that some of those emotions which made a glaring show, and were greatly admired by many, were in reality nothing, the devil sees it to be for his interest to work another way, and to endeavour to his utmost to propagate and establish a persuasion that all affections and emotions of the mind in religion are not to be regarded at all, but are rather to be avoided, and carefully guarded against, as things of a pernicious tendency. He knows this is the way to bring all religion to a mere lifeless formality, and effectually to shut out the power of godliness and everything spiritual. For although to true religion there must indeed be something else besides affection, yet true religion consists so much in the affections that there can be no true religion without them. He who has no religious affections is in a state of spiritual death, and is wholly destitute of the powerful, quickening, saving influences of the Spirit of God upon his heart. As there is not true religion where there is nothing else but affection, so there is no true religion where there is no religious affection. As on the one hand there must be light in the understanding, as well as an affected, fervent heart; or where there is heat without light, there can be nothing divine or heavenly in that heart; so, on the other hand, where there is a kind of light without heat, a head stored with notions and speculations with a cold and unaffected heart, there can be nothing divine in that light, that knowledge is no true spiritual knowledge of divine things. If the great things of religion are rightly understood, they will affect the heart. The reason why men are not affected by such infinitely great, important, glorious, and wonderful things as they often hear and read of in the word of God, is undoubtedly because they are blind. If they were not so, it would be impossible, and utterly inconsistent with human nature, that their hearts should be otherwise than strongly impressed and greatly moved by such things.

This manner of slighting all religious affections is the way exceedingly to harden the hearts of men, to encourage them in their stupidity and senselessness, to keep them in a state of spiritual death as long as they live, and bring them at last to death eternal.

The prevailing prejudice against religious affections at this day is apparently of awful effect to harden the hearts of sinners, to damp the graces of the saints, to preclude the effect of ordinances, and hold us down in a state of dullness and apathy; and this undoubtedly causes many people greatly to offend God, in entertaining mean and low thoughts of the extraordinary work he has recently done in this land. For people to despise and cry down all religious affections is the way to shut all religion out of their own hearts, and to make thorough work in ruining their souls.

Those who condemn high affection in others are certainly not likely to have high affections themselves. And let it be considered that those who have but little religious affection certainly have little religion. And those who condemn others for the religious affections, and have none themselves, have no religion. There are false affections, and there are true. A man's having much affection does not prove that he has any true religion, but if he has *no* affection it proves that he has no true religion. The right way is not to reject all affections, nor to approve all, but to distinguish between them, approving some and rejecting others; separating between the wheat and the chaff, the gold and the dross, the precious and the vile.

We should desire things that move the affections

If true religion lies much in the affections, we may infer that we are to desire such means as have much tendency to move the affections. Such books, and such a way of preaching the word and the administration of ordinances, and such a way of worshipping God in prayer and praises as has a tendency deeply to affect the hearts of those who attend these means, is much to be desired.

Such kind of means would formerly have been highly approved, and applauded by the generality of people as the most excellent and profitable, and having the greatest tendency to promote the ends of the means of grace. But the prevailing taste seems of late to be strangely altered: that feeling manner of praying and preaching which would formerly have been admired and extolled because it has such a tendency to move the affections, now immediately excites disgust in many people, and moves no other affections than those of displeasure and contempt.

Perhaps, formerly, the generality (at least of the common people) were in the extreme of looking too much to an affectionate address in public performances; but now a very great part of the people seem to have gone far to the opposite extreme. Indeed there may be such means as have a great tendency to stir up the passions of weak and ignorant people, and yet have none to benefit their souls; for though they may have a tendency to excite affections, they have little or none to excite *gracious* affections. But, undoubtedly, if the things of religion in the means used are treated according to their nature and exhibited truly, tending to convey just apprehensions and a right judgement of them, then the more they tend to move the affections the better.

We should be ashamed we are not more affected

If true religion lies much in the affections, we may learn what great cause we have to be ashamed and confounded before God, that we are no more affected with the great things of religion. It appears from what has been said that this arises from our having so little true religion.

God has given affections to mankind for the same purpose as that for which he has given all the faculties and principles of the human soul, namely that they might be subservient to man's chief end, and the great business for which God has created him, that is, the business of religion. And yet how common it is among mankind that their affections are much more exercised and engaged in other matters than in religion! In matters which concern men's worldly interest, their outward delights, their honour and reputation, and their natural relations, they have their desires eager, their appetites vehement, their love warm and affectionate, their zeal ardent; in these things their hearts are tender and sensitive, easily moved, deeply impressed, much concerned, very perceptibly affected, and greatly engaged; much depressed with grief at worldly losses, and highly raised with joy at worldly successes and prosperity. But how insensitive and unmoved are most men about the great things of another world! How dull are their affections! How heavy and hard their hearts in these matters! Here their love is cold, their desires languid, their zeal low, and their gratitude small. How they can sit and hear of the infinite height and depth and length and breadth of the love of God in Christ Jesus – of his giving his infinitely dear so to be offered up a sacrifice for the sins of men – and of the unparalleled love of the innocent, holy Lamb of God manifested in his dying agonies, his bloody sweat, his loud and bitter cries and bleeding heart – and all this for enemies, to redeem them from deserved, eternal burnings, and to bring to unspeakable and everlasting joy and glory; and yet be cold, heavy, insensitive, and regardless! Where are the exercises of our affections proper, if not here? What is it that more requires them? And what can be a fit occasion of their lively and vigorous exercise, if not such as this? Can anything greater and more important be set in our view? Anything more wonderful and surprising, or that concerns our interest more closely? Can we suppose that the wise Creator implanted such principles in our nature as the affections, to lie still on such an occasion as this? Can any Christian, who believes the truth of these things, entertain such thoughts?

If we ought ever to exercise our affections at all, and if the Creator has not unwisely constituted the human nature in making these principles a part of it, then they ought to be exercised about those objects which are most worthy of them. But is there anything in heaven or earth so worthy to be the objects of our admiration and love, our earnest and longing desires, hope, rejoicing, and fervent zeal, as those things which are held out to us in the gospel of Jesus Christ? There not only are things declared most worthy to affect us, but they are exhibited in the most affecting manner. The glory and beauty of the blessed Jehovah, which is most worthy in itself to be the object of our admiration and love, is there exhibited in the most affecting manner that can be conceived of; as it appears shining in all its lustre, in the face of an incarnate, infinitely loving, meek, compassionate, dying Redeemer. All the virtues of the Lamb of God, his humility, patience, meekness, submission, obedience, love, and compassion, are exhibited to our view in a manner the most tending to move our affections of any that can be imagined; for they all had their greatest trial, their highest exercise, and brightest manifestation, when he was in the most affecting circumstances; even when he was under his last sufferings, those unutterable and unparalleled sufferings which he endured from his tender love and pity to us. There, also, the hateful *nature* of our *sins* is manifested in the most affecting manner possible; as we see the dreadful effects of them, in what our Redeemer, who undertook to answer for us, suffered for them. And there we have the most affecting manifestations of God's *hatred* of sin, and his wrath and justice in punishing it; as we see his justice in the strictness and inflexibleness of it, and his wrath in its terribleness, in so dreadfully punishing our sins, in one who was infinitely dear to him, and loving to us. Thus has God disposed things in the affair of our redemption, and in his glorious dispensations revealed to us in the gospel, as though everything were purposely contrived in such a manner as to have the greatest possible tendency to reach our hearts in the most tender part, and move our affections most perceptibly and strongly. How great cause have we therefore to be humbled to the dust, that we are no more affected!

The peace which Christ
gives his true followers

Peace I leave with you, my peace I give unto you: not as the world giveth, give I unto you (John 14:27)

These words are part of a most affectionate and affecting discourse that Christ had with his disciples the same evening in which he was betrayed, knowing that he was to be crucified the next day. This discourse begins with John 13:31, and is continued to the end of chapter 16. Christ began his discourse after he partook of the passover with them, after he had instituted and administered the sacrament of the supper, and after Judas had gone out, and none were left but his true and faithful disciples; whom he now addresses as his dear children. This was the last discourse that Christ had with them before his death. As it was his parting discourse and, as it were, his dying discourse, so it is on many accounts the most remarkable we have recorded in our Bibles.

It is evident this discourse made a deep impression on the minds of the disciples; and we may suppose that it did so in a special manner on the mind of John, the beloved disciple, whose heart was especially full of love to him, and who had just then been leaning on his bosom. In this discourse Christ had told his dear disciples that he was going away, which filled them with sorrow and heaviness. The words of the text are given to comfort them, and to relieve their sorrow. He supports them with the promise of that peace which he would leave with them, and which they would have in him and with him when he had gone.

This promise he delivers in three emphatic expressions which illustrate one another. 'Peace I leave with you.' As much as to say, though I am going away, yet I will not take all comfort away with me. While I have been with you, I have been your support and comfort, and you have had peace in me in the midst of the losses you have sustained, and troubles you have met with from this evil generation. This peace I will not take from you, but leave it with you in a more full possession.

'My peace I give unto you.' Christ by calling it his peace signifies two things:

1. That it was his *own*, that which he had to give. It was the peculiar benefit that he had to bestow on his children, now he was about to leave the world as to his human presence. Silver and gold he had none; for, while in his state of humiliation, he was poor. The foxes had holes, and the birds of the air had nests, but the Son of man had not where to lay his head (Luke 9:58). He had no earthly estate to leave to his disciples who were as it were his family; but he had *peace* to give them.

2. It was *his* peace that he gave them, as it was the same kind of peace which he himself enjoyed. The same excellent and divine peace which he always had in God, and which he was about to receive in his exalted state in a vastly greater perfection and fullness: for the happiness Christ gives to his people is a participation in his own happiness: 'These things have I said unto you, that *my* joy might remain in you' (John 15:11). And in his prayer with his disciples at the conclusion of this discourse: 'And now come I to thee, and these things I speak in the world, that they might have my joy fulfilled in themselves . . . And the glory which thou gavest me, I have given them' (John 17:13, 22).

Christ here alludes to men making their wills before death. When parents are about to leave their children by death, they give them their estate in their last will and testament – the estate which they themselves used to possess and enjoy. So it was with Christ when he was about to leave the world, with respect to the peace which he gave his disciples; only with this difference, that earthly parents, when they die, though they leave the same estate to their children which they themselves have enjoyed up that point, yet when the children come to the full possession of it, they no longer enjoy it – the parents do not enjoy it with their children. Whereas with respect to Christ's peace, he did not only possess it himself before his death, when he bequeathed it to his disciples, but also afterwards more fully; so that they were received to possess it with him.

The third and last expression is, 'Not as the world giveth, give I unto you'. Which is as much as to say, my gifts and legacies, now I am going to leave the world, are not like those which the rich and great men of the world leave their heirs when they die. They bequeath their worldly possession to their children; and it may be, vast treasures of silver and gold, and sometimes an earthly kingdom. But the thing that I give you is my peace, a vastly different thing from what they give, and which cannot be obtained by all that they can bestow, or their children inherit from them.

Doctrine

That peace which Christ, when he died, left as a legacy to all his true saints is very different from all those things which the men of the world bequeath to their children when they die.

Christ's bequest

Christ at his death made over the blessings of the new covenant to believers as if in a will or testament. The new covenant is represented by the apostle as Christ's last will and testament. 'And for this cause he is the Mediator of the New Testament, that by means of death, for the redemption of the transgressions that were under the first testament, they which are called might receive the promise of eternal inheritance. For where a testament is, there must also of necessity be the death of the testator' (Hebrews 9:15-16). What men convey by their will or testament is their own estate. So Christ in the new covenant conveys to believers his own inheritance, so far as they are capable of possessing and enjoying it. They have that eternal life given to them in their measure which Christ himself possesses. They live in him, and with him, and by participating in his life. *Because he lives they live also.* They inherit his kingdom – the same kingdom which the Father appointed to him. 'And I appoint unto you a kingdom, as my Father hath appointed unto me' (Luke 22:29). They will reign on his throne (Revelation 3:21). They have his glory given to them (John 17). And because all things are Christ's, so in Christ all things are the saints' (1 Corinthians 3:21-22).

Men in their wills or testaments most commonly give their estates to their children; similarly, believers are represented in Scripture as Christ's children. 'Behold, I, and the children which God hath given me' (Hebrews 2:13). Men most commonly make their wills a little before their death; so Christ, in a very special and solemn manner, made over and confirmed to his disciples the blessings of the new covenant, on the evening before the day of his crucifixion, in that discourse of which my text is a part. The promises of the new covenant were never so particularly expressed, and so solemnly given by Christ in all the time that he was on earth, as in this discourse. Christ promises them mansions in his Father's house (16:1-3). Here he promises them whatever blessings they would need and ask in his name (15:7; 14:23-24). Here he more solemnly and fully than anywhere else gives and confirms the promise of the Holy Spirit, which is the sum of the blessings of the covenant of grace (14:18; 17:26; 15:25; 16:7). Here he promises them his own and his Father's gracious presence and favour (14:18; 19:20-21). Here he promises them peace (14:27). Here he promises them his joy (15:11). Here he promises grace to bring forth holy fruits (15:16), and victory over the world (16:33). And indeed there seems to be nowhere else so full and complete an edition of the covenant of grace in the whole Bible as in this dying discourse of Christ with his eleven true disciples.

This covenant between Christ and his children is like a will or testament also in this respect, that it becomes effectual, and a way is made for putting it in execution, no other way than by his death; as the apostle observes it is with a will or testament among men. 'For a testament is of force after men are dead' (Hebrews 9:17). For though the covenant of grace indeed was of force before the death of Christ, yet it was of force in no other way than by his death; so that his death then did virtually intervene, being already under-taken and engaged. As a man's heirs come by the legacies bequeathed to them in no other way than by the death of the testator, so men come by the spiritual and eternal inheritance in no other way than by the death of Christ. If it had not been for the death of Christ they could never have obtained it.

The peace of Christ

A great blessing that Christ in his testament has bequeathed to his true followers is his peace. Here I would particularly observe two things:

True peace

Our Lord Jesus Christ has bequeathed true peace and comfort to his followers. Christ is called the Prince of peace (Isaiah 9:6). And when he was born into the world, the angels on that joyful and wonderful occasion sang, 'Glory to God in the highest, on earth *peace*' – because of that peace which he would procure for and bestow on the children of men; peace with God, and peace with one another, and tranquillity and peace within themselves. The last is especially the benefit spoken about in the text. This Christ has procured for his followers, and laid a foundation for their enjoy-ment of it, in that he has procured for them the other two, namely, peace with God and peace with one another. He has procured for them peace and reconciliation with God, and his favour and friendship; in satisfaction of their sins, and laying a foundation for the perfect removal of the guilt of sin, and the forgiveness of all their trespasses, and working out for them a perfect and glorious righteousness, most acceptable to God, and sufficient to recommend them to God's full acceptance, to the adoption of children, and to the eternal fruits of his father's kindness.

By these means true saints are brought into a state of freedom from condemnation, and all the curses of the law of God: 'Who is he that condemneth?' (Romans 8:34). And by these means they are safe from that dreadful and eternal misery to which they are naturally exposed, and are set in high out of reach of all their enemies, so that the gates of hell and powers of darkness can never destroy them; nor can wicked men ever hurt them, though they may persecute. 'If God be for us, who can be against us?' (Romans 8:31). 'How shall I curse whom God hath not cursed? . . . There is no enchantment against Jacob, neither is there any divination against Israel' (Numbers 23:8, 23). By these means they are out of the reach of death: 'This is the bread which cometh down from heaven, that a man may eat thereof and not die' (John 6:50). By these means death with respect to them has lost its sting, and is no more worthy of the name of death. 'O death, where is thy sting?' (1 Corinthians 15:55). By these means they have no need to be afraid of the day of judgement, when the heavens and earth are dissolved. 'God is our refuge and strength, a very present help in trouble. Therefore will not we fear, though the earth be removed: and though the mountains be carried into the midst of the sea' (Psalm 46:1-2). Indeed, a true saint has reason to be at rest in an assurance that nothing can separate him from the love of God (Romans 8:38-39).

Thus anyone who is in Christ is in a safe refuge from everything that might disturb him: 'And a man shall be as an hiding place from the wind, and a covert from the tempest: as rivers of water in a dry place, as the shadow of a great rock in a weary land' (Isaiah 32:2). And hence those who dwell in Christ have that promise fulfilled to them: 'And my people shall dwell in a peaceable habitation, and in sure dwellings, and in quiet resting-places' (Isaiah 33:18).

And the true followers of Christ have not only ground of rest and peace of soul, by reason of their safety from evil, but on account of their sure title and certain enjoyment of all that good which they stand in need of, living, dying, and through all eternity. They are on a sure foundation for happiness, are built on a rock that can never be moved, and have a fountain that is sufficient, and can never be exhausted. The covenant is ordered in all things and sure, and God has passed his word and oath that 'by two immutable things, in which it was impossible for God to lie, we might have strong consolation, who have fled for refuge to lay hold on the hope set before us'. The infinite Jehovah has become their God, and can do everything for them. He who is their portion has an infinite fullness of good in himself. 'He is their shield and exceeding great reward.' As *great* a good is made over to them as they can desire or conceive of; and is made as *sure* as they can desire: therefore they have reason to put their hearts at rest, and be at peace in their minds.

Besides, he has bequeathed peace to the souls of his people, as he has procured for them and made over to them the spirit of grace and true holiness; which has a natural tendency to the peace and quietness of the soul. It implies a discovery and relish of a suitable and sufficient good. It brings a person into a view of divine beauty, and to a relish of that good which is a man's proper happiness; and so it brings the soul to its true centre. The soul by his means is brought to rest, and ceases from restlessly inquiring, as others do, who will show us any good; and wandering to and fro, like lost sheep seeking rest and finding none. The soul has found him who is the appletree among the trees of the wood, and sits down under his shadow with great delight, and his fruit is sweet to his taste (Song of Songs 2:2). And thus that saying of Christ is fulfilled: 'Whoever drinketh of the water that I shall give him, shall never thirst' (John 4:14). And besides, true grace naturally tends to peace and quietness, as it settles things in the soul in their due order, sets reason on the throne, and subjects the senses and affections to its government, which before were uppermost. Grace tends to tranquillity, as it mortifies tumultuous desires and passions, subdues the eager and insatiable appetites of the sensual nature and greediness after the vanities of the world. It mortifies such principles as hatred, variance, emulation, wrath, envyings, and the like, which are a continual source of inward uneasiness and perturbation; and supplies those sweet, calming, and quieting principles of humility, meekness, resignation, patience, gentleness, forgiveness, and sweet reliance on God. It also tends to peace, as it fixes the aim of the soul to a certain end; so that the soul is no longer distracted and drawn by opposite ends to be sought, and opposite portions to be obtained, and many masters of contrary wills and commands to be served; but the heart is fixed in the choice of one certain, sufficient, and unfailing good: and the soul's aim at this, and hope of it, is like an anchor that keeps it steadfast, that it should no more be driven to and fro by every wind.

Christ's own peace

This peace which Christ has left as a legacy to his true followers is his peace. It is the peace which he himself enjoys. This is what I take to be principally intended in the expression. It is the peace that he enjoyed while on earth, in his state of humiliation. Though he was a man of sorrows, and acquainted with grief, and was everywhere hated and persecuted by men and devils, and had no place of rest in this world; yet in God, his Father, he had peace. We read of his rejoicing in spirit (Luke 10:21). So Christ's true disciples, though in the world they have tribulation, yet in God have peace. 'When Christ had finished his labours and sufferings, had risen from the dead, and ascended into heaven, he entered into his rest, a state of most blessed, perfect, and everlasting peace: delivered by his own sufferings from our imputed guilt, acquitted and justified by the Father on his resurrection. Having obtained a perfect victory over all his enemies, he was received by his Father into heaven, the rest which he had prepared for him, there to enjoy his heart's desire fully and perfectly to all eternity. And then were the words of Psalm 21:1-6 fulfilled, which refer to Christ. This peace and rest of the Messiah is exceedingly glorious: 'And his rest shall be glorious' (Isaiah 11:10). This rest is what Christ has procured, not only for himself but also for his people, by his death; and he has bequeathed it to them, that they may enjoy it with him, imperfectly in this world, and perfectly and eternally in another.

That peace which has been described, and which believers enjoy, is a participation in the peace which their glorious Lord and Master himself enjoys, by virtue of the same blood by which Christ himself has entered into rest. It is in a participation in this same justification, for believers are justified with Christ. As he was justified when he rose from the dead, and as he was made free from our guilt, which he had as our surety, so believers are justified in him and through him as being accepted by God in the same righteousness. It is in the favour of the same God and heavenly Father that they enjoy peace. 'I ascend to my Father and your Father, to my God and your God.' It is in a participation in the same Spirit; for believers have the Spirit of Christ. He had the Spirit given to him not by measure, and of his fullness do they all receive, and grace for grace. As the oil poured on the head of Aaron went down to the skirts of his garments, so the Spirit poured on Christ, the head, descends to all his members. It is as partaking of the same grace of the Spirit that believers enjoy this peace (John 1:16).

It is in being united to Christ, and living by a participation in his life, as a branch lives by the life of the vine. It is as partaking of the same love of God: 'That the love wherewith thou hast loved me may be in them' (John 17:26). It is as having a part with him in his victory over the same enemies; and also as having an interest in the same kind of eternal rest and peace. 'Even when we were dead in sins, hath quickened us together with Christ . . . and hath raised us up together, and hath made us sit together in heavenly places' (Ephesians 2:5-6).

A different kind of legacy

This legacy of Christ to his true disciples is very different from all the men of this world ever leave to their children when they die. The men of this world, many of them, when they come to die, have great estates to bequeath to their children, an abundance of the good things of this world, large tracts of ground, perhaps in a fruitful soil, covered with flocks and herds. They sometimes leave to their children stately mansions, and vast treasures of silver, gold, jewels, and precious things, fetched from both the Indies, and from every side of the globe. They leave them the means to live in much state and magnificence, and make a great show among men, to fare very sumptuously, and swim in worldly pleasures. Some have crowns, sceptres, and palaces, and great monarchies to leave to their heirs. But none of these things are to be compared to that blessed peace of Christ which he has bequeathed to his true followers. These things are such as God commonly in his providence gives his worst enemies, those whom he hates and despises most. But Christ's peace is a precious benefit, which he reserves for his special favourites. These worldly things, even the best of them, that the men and princes of the world leave for their children, are things which God in his providence throws out to those whom he looks on as dogs; but Christ's peace is the bread of his children. All these earthly things are but empty shadows, which, however men set their hearts on them, are not bread, and can never satisfy their souls; but this peace of Christ is a truly substantial satisfying food (Isaiah 55:2). None of those things, if men have them to the best advantage, can give true peace and rest to the soul, as is abundantly clear not only in reason, but experience; for it is found in all ages that those who have the most of them have commonly the least quietness of mind. It is true, there may be a kind of quietness, a false peace, in the enjoyment of worldly things; men may bless their souls, and think themselves the only happy persons, and despise others; they may say to their souls, as the rich man did, 'Soul, thou has much goods laid up for many years, take thine ease, eat, drink, and be merry' (Luke 12:19). But Christ's peace, which he gives to his true disciples, differs from this peace that men may have in the enjoyments of the world, in the following respects:

It is rational

Christ's peace is a rational peace and rest of soul: it is what has its foundation in light and knowledge, in the proper exercise of reason, and a right view of things; whereas the peace of the world is founded in blindness and delusion. The peace that the people of Christ have arises from their having their eyes open, and seeing things as they are. The more they consider, and the more they know of the truth and reality of things – the more they know what is true concerning themselves, the state and condition they are in; the more they know of God, and what manner of being he is; the more certain they are of another world and future judgement, and of the truth of God's threats and promises; the more their consciences are awakened and enlightened, and the brighter and the more searching the light – the more is their peace established. Whereas, on the contrary, the peace that the men of the world have in their worldy enjoyments can subsist in no other way than by their being kept in ignorance. They must by blindfolded and deceived, otherwise they can have no peace: if the light is only let in upon their consciences, so that they may look about them and see what they are, and what circumstances they are in, it will at once destroy all their quietness and comfort. Their peace can live nowhere but in the dark. Light turns their ease into torment. The more they know what is true concerning God and concerning themselves, the more they are aware of the truth concerning those enjoyments which they possess; and the more they are aware what things now are, and what things are likely to be hereafter, the more will their calm be turned into a storm. The worldly man's peace cannot be maintained except by avoiding thinking about things or reflecting. If he allows himself to think, and properly to exercise his reason, it destroys his quietness and comfort. If he wants to establish his carnal peace, it concerns him to put out the light of his mind, and turn beast as fast as he can. The faculty of reason, if at liberty,

175

proves a mortal enemy to his peace. It concerns him, if he wants to keep his peace alive, to stupefy his mind and deceive himself, and to imagine things to be otherwise than they are. But with respect to the peace which Christ gives, reason is its great friend. The more this faculty is exercised, the more it is established. The more they consider and view things with truth and exactness, the firmer is their comfort and the higher their joy. How vast a difference then there is between the peace of a Christian and the worldling! How miserable are those who cannot enjoy any peace except by hiding their eyes from the light, and confining themselves to darkness. Their peace is stupidity; it is the ease that a man has who has taken a dose of stupefying poison, the ease and pleasure that a drunkard may have in a house on fire over his head, or the joy of a distracted man in thinking that he is a king, though a miserable wretch confined in bedlam! Whereas the peace the Christ gives his true disciples is the light of life, something of the tranquillity of heaven, the peace of the celestial paradise that has the glory of God to lighten it.

It is virtuous and holy

The peace that the men of the world enjoy is vicious: it is vile, depraves and debases the mind, and makes men brutish. But the peace that the saints enjoy in Christ is not only their comfort, but it is a part of their beauty and dignity. The Christian tranquillity, rest, and joy of real saints are not only unspeakable privileges, but they are virtues and graces of God's Spirit, in which his image partly consists. This peace has its source in those principles which are in the highest degree virtuous and amiable, such as poverty of spirit, holy resignation, trust in God, divine love, meekness, and charity; the exercise of the blessed fruits of the Spirit (Galatians 5:22-23).

It is sweet

This peace greatly differs from that which is enjoyed by the men of the world, with regard to its exquisite sweetness. It is a peace so much above all that natural men enjoy in wordly things, that it surpasses their understanding and conception (Philippians 4:7). It is exquisitely sweet and secure, because it has so firm a foundation, the everlasting rock that can never be moved; because it is perfectly consistent with reason; because it rises from holy and divine principles, that, as they are the virtue, so are they the proper happiness of men; and because the greatness of the objective good that the saints enjoy is no other than the infinite bounty and fulness of that God who is the fountain of all good. The fullness and perfection of that provision that is made in Christ and the new covenant is a foundation laid for the saints' perfect peace; and this hereafter they will actually enjoy. And though their peace is not now perfect, it is not owing to any defect in the provision made, but to their own imperfection, sin, and darkness. As yet, they partly cleave to the world, and seek peace from there, and do not perfectly cleave to Christ. But the more they do so, and the more they seek of the provision made, and accept it, and cleave to that alone, the nearer are they brought to perfect tranquillity (Isaiah 26:5).

It is eternal

The peace of the Christian infinitely differs from that of the worldling, in that it is unfailing and eternal. That peace which carnal men have in the things of the world is, according to the foundation upon which it is built, of short continuance; like the comfort of a dream (1 John 2; 1 Corinthians 7:31). These things, the best and most durable of them, are like bubbles on the face of the water; they vanish in a moment (Hosea 10:7). But the foundation of the Christian's peace is everlasting; it is what no time, no change, can destroy. It will remain when the body dies: it will remain when the mountains depart and the hills are removed, and when the heavens are rolled together like a scroll. The fountain of his comfort will never be diminished, and the stream will never be dried. His comfort and joy is a living spring in the soul, a well of water springing up to everlasting life.

Application

The use I would make of this doctrine is to make it an inducement to all to forsake the world, no longer seeking peace and rest in its vanities, and to cleave to Christ and follow him. Happiness and rest are what all men pursue. But the things of the world, where most men seek it, can never give it; they are labouring and spending themselves in vain. But Christ invites you to come to him, and offers you this peace which he gives his true followers, and that so much excels all that the world can afford (Isaiah 55:2-3).

You that have hitherto spent your time in the pursuit of satisfaction in the profit or glory of the world, or in the pleasures and vanities of youth, have this day an offer of that excellent and everlasting peace and blessedness which Christ has purchased with the price of his own blood. As long as you continue to reject those offers and invitations of Christ, and continue in a Christless condition, you never will enjoy any true peace or comfort; but will be like the prodigal, who in vain endeavoured to be satisfied with the husks that the swine ate. The wrath of God will abide upon you, and misery will attend you, wherever you go, and you will never be able to escape it. Christ gives peace to the most sinful and miserable that come to him. He heals the broken in heart and binds up their wounds. But it is impossible for people to have peace while they continue in their sins (Isaiah 57:19-21). There is no peace between God and them; for, as they have the guilt of sin remaining in their souls, and are under its dominion, so God's indignation continually burns against them, and therefore they travail in pain all their days. While you continue in such a state, you live in dreadful uncertainty what will become of you, and in continual danger. When you are in the enjoyment of things most pleasing to you, where your heart is best suited and most cheerful, you are still in a state of condemnation. You hang over the infernal pit, with the sword of divine vengeance hanging over your head, having no security one moment from utter and remediless destruction. What reasonable peace can anyone enjoy in such a state as this? What though you clothe him in gorgeous apparel, or set him on a throne, or at a prince's table, and feed him with the rarest dainties the earth affords? How miserable is the ease and cheerfulness that such people have! What a poor kind of comfort and joy it is that such people take in their wealth and pleasures for a moment, while they are the prisoners of divine justice, and wretched captives of the devil! They have no one to befriend them, being without Christ, aliens from commonwealth of Israel, strangers from the covenant of promise, having no hope, and without God in the world!

I invite you now to a better portion. There are better things provided for the sinful, miserable children of men. There is a surer comfort and more durable peace: comfort that you may enjoy in a state of safety, and on a sure foundation: a peace and rest that you may enjoy with reason, and with your eyes open. You may have all your sins forgiven, your greatest and most aggravated transgressions blotted out as a cloud, and buried as in the depths of the sea, that they may never be found again. And being not only forgiven, but accepted to favour, you become the objects of God's delight; being taken into God's family and made his children, you may have good evidence that your names were written on the heart of Christ before the world was made, and that you have an interest in all things and sure; wherein is promised no less than life and immortality, an inheritance incorruptible and undefiled, a crown of glory that does not fade away. Being in such circumstances, nothing will be able to prevent your being happy to all eternity; having for the foundation of your hope that love of God which is from eternity to eternity; and his promise and oath, and his omnipotent power, things infinitely firmer than mountains of brass. The mountains will depart, and the hills be removed, even the heavens will vanish away like smoke, and the earth will grow old like a garment, yet these things will never be abolished.

In such a state as this you will have a foundation of peace and rest through all changes, and in times of the greatest uproar and outward calamity be defended from all storms, and dwell above the floods (Psalm 32:6-70). And you will be at peace with everything, and God will make all his creatures throughout all parts of his dominion befriend you (Job 5:19-24). You need not be afraid of anything that your enemies can do to you (Psalm 3:5-6). The things that now are most terrible to you, namely death, judgement, and eternity, will then be most comfortable, the most sweet and pleasant objects of your contemplation – or at least there will be reason why they should be so. Listen therefore to the friendly counsel that is given you this day, turn your feet into the way of peace, forsake the foolish and live; forsake those things that are nothing other than the devil's baits, and seek after this excellent peace and rest of Jesus Christ, that peace of God which passes all understanding. Taste and see; no one who ever tried it was disappointed (Proverbs 24:13-14). You will not only find those spiritual comforts that Christ offers you to be of a surpassing sweetness for the present, but they will be to your soul like the dawning light that shines more and more to the perfect day; and the result will be your arrival in heaven, that land of rest, those regions of everlasting joy, where your peace and happiness will be perfect, without the least mixture of trouble or affliction, and never be interrupted nor have an end.

Books by
Jonathan Edwards

An account of the life of Rev. David Brainerd. Boston, 1749

A careful and strict enquiry into the modern prevailing notions of freedom of will. Boston, 1754

Charity and its fruits. New York, 1851

A faithful narrative of the surprising work of God in the conversion of many hundred souls in Northampton, and the neighbouring towns. London, 1737

God glorified in the work of redemption, by the greatness of man's dependence upon him: a sermon preached in Boston, July 8, 1731. Boston, 1731

The great Christian doctrine of original sin defended. Boston, 1758

A history of the work of redemption: containing the outline of a body of divinity. Edinburgh, 1774

A humble attempt to promote explicit agreement and visible union of God's people in extraordinary prayer for the revival of religion and the advancement of Christ's kingdom on earth. Boston, 1747

A humble inquiry into the rules of the word of God, concerning the qualifications requisite to a compleat standing and full communion in the visible Christian church. Boston, 1749

Miscellaneous observations on important theological subjects, original and collected. Edinburgh, 1793

Misrepresentations corrected, and truth vindicated: in a reply to the Rev. Solomon William's book, The true state of the question concerning the qualifications necessary to lawful communion in the Christian sacraments. Boston, 1752

Remarks on important theological controversies. Edinburgh, 1796

The resort and remedy of those that are bereaved by the death of an eminent minister: a sermon preached at the interment of the Rev. Mr. William Williams. Boston, 1741

Sermons on various important subjects. In Samuel Hopkins, *Life and character,* Boston, 1765

Some thoughts concerning the present revival of religion in New-England, and the way in which it ought to be acknowledged and promoted. Boston, 1742

A treatise concerning religious affections. Boston, 1746

True saints, when absent from the body, are present with the Lord: a sermon preached on the day of the funeral of the Rev. Mr. David Brainerd. Boston, 1747

Two dissertations. I. Concerning the end for which God created the world. II. The nature of true virtue. Boston, 1765

Works. London, 1834. 2 vols.

Works. New Haven: Yale University Press, 1957.